The Model

Valerie Lee J

authorHOUSE®

AuthorHouse™
1663 Liberty Drive
Bloomington, IN 47403
www.authorhouse.com
Phone: 1-800-839-8640

Published by AuthorHouse 9/18/2013

ISBN: 978-1-4772-7177-3 (sc)
ISBN: 978-1-4817-3521-6 (hc)
ISBN: 978-1-4772-7176-6 (e)

Library of Congress Control Number: 2012917364

Allison Randall was sitting at her desk. She thought about her daughter Lynn. Her daughter was ten years old. Lynn planned to begin in a new class. She learned new things every day. One of Lynn's favorite things to do was draw.

Allison and her daughter completed activities together. Allison enjoyed spending time with her daughter.

As Allison drove the car in the drive next door, she wanted to finalize the plans with Lynn for the weekend.

Jean greeted Allison.

"Lynn has been waiting on you to arrive. She has been gone away from home all day. We managed to keep ourselves busy for, several, hours, after her school day ended. Lynn and I had a great time today".

"Do you think that you will bring her to visit me, even when she begins her new school year? I know that you do not work as many hours as in the past".

Allison promised Jean, that she would bring Lynn to visit.

Allison came inside the home of Jean.

Lynn approached Allison.

"Allison, I did have a good time today with Ms. Anders".

For some reason, her daughter called Allison, by her first name.

As a young girl, Lynn realized that her parents were divorced. Lynn talked with Edgar often, and had known that he was dating a colleague in the peace organization he was involved with. The peace organization was involved with assisting relief to people.

The last that Allison knew, was that the organization was completing work in another town. Edgar had written a letter to Lynn, not long before.

Jean acknowledged Lynn, as she told her, that she would, see her the next day.

Lynn waved to the woman.

Jean stood outside her front door, and watched, Allison, and Lynn leave.

"Allison, I wonder what Edgar is doing at this time. I know that he is part of an organization assisting relief to people".

Lynn had been correct. Lynn and Edgar enjoyed spending time together.

"You will be able to talk with him soon".

Allison told her daughter, that they could go out for lunch, that weekend.

"We can visit the restaurant that is not far, from our home".

Allison told Lynn, about the restaurant, as they drove to a small boutique to buy a suit that Allison decided that she would buy. Allison thought that it would be nice to wear the suit to work in the future.

"We are here".

Lynn opened her door. Allison and Lynn walked inside the boutique together. Lynn was young, and had not shared the same ideas of wardrobe pieces, as Allison. Lynn preferred jeans, and a shirt.

For the time of year, the weather was warm.

Lynn walked along side of Allison. Her mother bought a new selection for her wardrobe, every so often.

When they arrived home, Allison and Lynn together, read, several, articles in the newspaper. Allison searched through real estate listings, to see if there were any updates.

The next morning, Allison and Lynn drove to the restaurant that was not far from their home. They ordered tea. Allison and Lynn had not noticed the crowd around them.

Lynn thought for a moment, before she talked.

"I know that you enjoy your career in real estate. You are constantly getting details together for clients".

Lynn had been thinking back to past conversations with Allison. She had been correct. Allison had not minded being involved with real estate.

Lynn was talkative, as she continued. She told Allison, that she wanted to become an artist. Lynn enjoyed being creative. There were not many neighbors that Allison and Lynn knew, besides Jean. They recognized faces of people that lived in the nearby homes.

Allison has told her daughter in the past, how Edgar and she met. After going to similar places with mutual acquaintances, they began dating. Edgar and Allison decided to marry, and Allison found that she had been pregnant with Lynn.

"Lynn, I think that one day you will decide to become married".

Allison hoped that her daughter would understand that the ideas they had of living their lives, had grown Allison and Edgar apart. She knew at times, her daughter was concerned about her parents. Allison had not thought about dating at this time. After a while, Allison and Lynn left the restaurant.

Allison recalled in her mind the photos of her family that she placed on her desk at work. Some of her colleagues at the office knew of her previous relationship.

Allison often heard her colleagues talk of their relationships with their spouses or their partners.

There was a realtor in the office that recently had a child, after being married for, several, years.

It had been Monday. It had been the first day of the work week. The office was busy, that day. Allison's colleagues were talking with prospective clients on the phone.

Allison had begun processing real estate loans, after she stopped selling real estate. The processing of real estate loans had not been over whelming for her. There were, few, people that wanted to work with the demands of real estate. The work primarily consisted of individuals buying property.

Years ago, Allison would not have imagined herself working in real estate. Allison imagined herself being a gown designer.

Allison went through most of the day talking to clients on the phone. She took a break midafternoon.

Allison attended school not far from the town that she lived in with her daughter. Lynn adjusted to the house, that Allison and Lynn now lived in.

Lynn reminded Allison over the weekend that Allison had to make arrangements for her to begin classes for the upcoming school year.

There had been a car that crossed in front of Allison. She made a left turn. Allison barely missed colliding with the vehicle.

Allison talked with the secretary of the school. Moments later, Allison completed the necessary documents. She had given the secretary the necessary information.

"The process to register children for school is not difficult".

The secretary told Allison the name of the teacher with the particular class. The teacher had not been at the building at the time, for Allison to meet her.

After the meeting, Allison went to the home of Jean.

"We have been waiting for you, as usual. I had two past acquaintances that were in town. They spent part of the day with Lynn and me. They moved from the home, several, years ago. We were neighbors for a while. They wanted to live in a different part of town. They wanted to be closer to their family. We were neighbors, before I decided to move here. I have not gone to visit them. They had another acquaintance that they recently visited, that lives in the city".

Allison had never met the individuals that Jean had been referring to.

Allison knew that Jean was close to her family. She often talked about her family. They lived quite a distance away from Jean. She has told Allison, that the next time she visited her family, that Lynn and she were welcomed to come with her.

Allison had no idea when the trip would be planned.

Allison began to tell Jean about the recent incident near the office. A doctor had been mugged. It occurred not far from the building. The doctor had been a specialist. The incident happened, after he had been late coming out of his office.

At times, incidents happened throughout the town. Allison knew that there would be individuals that would be concerned for a while about the mugging and robbery of the doctor.

Allison continued the conversation.

"I would drive, several, miles from the gown boutique that I worked for. The designer had become even more popular, since I stopped working for her. Sara asked me to take care of the store if she left out of town. There was a time that Sara told me she had to meet with, several, executives. This was before, Sara had become known throughout the city. She had been my favorite employer for the five years that I worked for her. Sara would always wear the same black scarf around her shoulders. I do not think I' am as creative with designing, as she".

At home, Allison made, several, calls. Allison had to respond to, several, messages from earlier that day, when she had been at the office. By the end of her calls, Allison organized several, appointments. Several hours, went by, quickly, that evening.

An hour later, Allison watched Lynn draw.

"Allison, I drew this for you. It reminded me of a dress we saw the other day. We visit different boutiques".

6

Allison knew that her daughter would soon have acquaintances in the class. Allison had been glad that Lynn enjoyed spending time with Edgar and her. Allison knew that Edgar wanted to continue to spend time with his daughter, because Lynn meant a lot to him.

That morning, Allison talked with, several, people on the phone. Allison thought that her morning had gone smoothly.

At noon exactly, Allison walked away from the office building. She decided to walk along the store fronts. Allison looked at the clothing designs, for the upcoming season.

Allison noticed a gentleman starring at her. She ignored him, as she continued to walk. The gentleman walked toward Allison, and before he reached her, he turned around. Allison had not wanted to panic. When Allison turned around again, the gentleman remained gone.

Allison had been thinking of Lynn, and the time they spend together. She decided to go inside the restaurant.

Allison ordered a warmed tea.

Allison had gone inside the restaurant, several, times in the past. She had been visiting the restaurant, since the three years, she had been with Delkes Realty. Allison knew that many people, thought working for a real estate company was fast paced, and, that it was difficult to keep the attention of clients.

The colleagues that Allison now works with are not the same. Her colleagues continue to make it easy for her to work with the clients that the office had.

Allison sat quietly reading the menu at the restaurant.

Everyone, inside the office, was busy, by midafternoon. Mark came by Allison's desk.

"Allison, I' am unsure how you manage to balance your work. The clients keep me busy. They want constant updates on their files.

I' am not particular which real estate office I work for. This firm is productive".

"We all have our families to keep us busy. I worry about David, while I' am at the office during the day. He began school last year, and he is adjusting. Gillian and I are glad that he is growing up. David has begun to remember a lot of details around him".

Allison could understand what Mark meant.

Allison starred at the work in front of her. There were documents that needed to be completed.

"I will be glad if I' am able to get these loans processed. Then, I have to have the meetings with the real estate agents, and the clients. They never take long".

Mark left Allison alone to complete her work.

By the time Allison finished her work, some of the loans were unable to be completed. There were reasons the contracts had not been completed. Several, of the clients had become confused on the amount of interest that they were responsible for. The clients were looking forward to different homes.

Allison completed her work for the day. She completed her work well. People often complemented her on her work.

When Lynn was born, Allison became more focused on raising her daughter.

Allison met with a client at a restaurant.

"This restaurant is nice. It reminds me of the restaurant my husband works for. I' am able to try different foods at home, on an occasion. My husband enjoys culinary. He has worked in restaurants for a number of years. When he is home, he tries different recipes that he wants to use at the restaurant. He does work long hours".

"We have been thinking about buying a different house for, several, years".

The woman held her young daughter in her arms.

"Maureen is almost two. I hope that we have not taken up too much of your time with the prospect of the house. The process of buying a house can be lengthy".

The woman continued to talk about her family.

Allison and the woman held a conversation for, several, minutes, before Allison ended the meeting.

Allison reminded the woman, that she had a different meeting with another client. Allison assured the woman, that everything would be fine with purchasing the house. Allison knew that everything would close on the family's current home, and go as expected.

Allison found her way to the meeting.

Allison arrived, and located a home that was on a road not far from the interstate. The door opened, as she came into the drive.

"I have been waiting for you. We had not expected to get a lower interest rate, than we had on this home. Maryanne and I need a larger house, since we now have my parents living with us. They are older, but they do need our attention".

The gentleman looked, as if he could not have been older, than his fifties.

"Maryanne is at work, but we thought it might be a good idea if I met with you to show our interest in the house".

Allison and the gentleman sat in the kitchen.

"My parents are living in their current home".

Allison liked the design of the kitchen.

Allison removed the documents. Allison began to explain some details about the loan the family had chosen.

"I know that you tried the best that you could. The interest on the loan is what we expected it to be".

Allison assured the gentleman, that with the information they provided, the contract would not be much different than when they purchased the current home. They continued to talk for a while. They had been together for over an hour. The only noise was that of them rustling paper, and their voices.

After the hour, the gentleman offered Allison coffee. They remained on their task until he signed, and initialed the documents in, several, areas.

At dusk, Allison told the gentleman that she needed to return home to her daughter. She was waiting for her at the home of their neighbor.

"The purchase of this house is a great idea".

The gentleman was dressed, as if he had gone to an office that day. The gentleman had given Allison a handshake, before she left. He had been glad that things would go well.

When Allison arrived home, she searched through files. Lynn was drawing, since she had completed her assignment. Lately, spending time together had been their routine.

Allison had taken time off from real estate, when she began assisting Sara in her gown boutique. A year after Lynn was born Allison had been well into her career, as a loan processor.

When Allison arrived to the office, Mark told her about a recent incident near the office.

"I' am sure everyone is being more cautious. I do not think anyone in town, could answer, why there had been incidents, happening, near the office building. I have been keeping my car parked close to the building".

Mark mentioned that he was teaching David how to ride a bike.

"At first, he was, having difficulty".

Mark and Allison held their conversation. Their conversation ended, when Allison noticed the documents lying on her desk.

Allison had taken, several, calls from prospective clients.

Allison had been on a call, when her door opened. It was Mary. She was the secretary at the office.

"There are individuals from the police department with an ambulance downstairs near the front entrance. A person driving had been hurt. The police asked that everyone remain cautious leaving the building".

Mary reminded them that the police apologized for any inconvenience.

It had been near one thirty.

Mark walked toward Allison.

"I have a meeting out today. I hope that everything is fine with the situation outside. No one would miss me at the office today".

Allison had a scheduled meeting. It was scheduled in, several, hours.

"Maybe, I will visit with Lynn for, several, hours before my meeting".

Allison and Mark walked to the parking lot. They walked in the direction toward the front of the building, to avoid the commotion outside.

Mark talked about his son. His son had been in a new class.

"He likes learning in class".

Allison found her daughter outside running through the grass throwing a Frisbee toward Zealand. He had been important to Jean. Allison could remember Jean telling her that she bought him, several, years before, when he had been young.

"It is nice that he is having a great time. He is becoming older, and I hope that he does not intimidate you. Lynn and you are the people he is around a lot. I bought Zealand, because growing up I was used to having pets around. Although I have to say, my older brother spent more time taking care of them than I had".

Lynn noticed her mother, and walked toward her.

"Are we leaving"?

Allison told Lynn, that they were going to buy something for the new class in, several, weeks.

Lynn agreed.

Lynn and Allison began walking toward the car.

By the time that Allison brought Lynn to Jean, Lynn had been carrying, a school bag full of school supplies. Lynn had been content.

Allison had enjoyed spending time with her daughter the day before. They liked completing activities together.

Allison waved, as she drove the car out of the drive. Allison mentally prepared in her mind, of the meeting that day. She never had any idea how long they would last. Earlier, Allison made a call to the woman about their meeting. They planned to meet at her gown boutique.

"I enjoy designing gowns. Allison, I have been designing for half my life".

The woman asked Allison, if she knew anything about designing gowns.

Allison told the woman the previous experience that she had with assisting Sara. It was different from the career she was doing at this time.

"Allison, if you had more time, I would ask you to assist me with my designs. There was a woman that wanted to assist me, but she began working with someone else. There are other people that assist me with my designs. They are with me on a limited basis".

Allison knew that the woman had been in business for a while. They were inside a boutique with, several, gowns. There had been photographs on the wall, of events, and individuals that had been wearing the designer's gowns. Allison had not had time to look through the designs of the gowns. Instead, Allison waited until the woman signed the necessary document. Allison left after finishing her coffee.

Allison called the office to be sure, that someone was there that morning.

When Allison arrived to the office, everything was usual.

Mark mentioned about the details from the previous afternoon. He had become even more familiar with the part of town.

"I hope, the gentleman, that had been hurt the previous afternoon, will be out of the hospital soon. I would not want to be in that situation. There are other areas in this town. Incidents are occurring near the office".

The phone began ringing.

Mark walked over to his desk to answer it.

Allison continued with her work. She planned to be in and out of the office, that day. The next day, Allison planned to bring Lynn to her first day of class. Lynn had already begun to ask Allison questions about school. Allison assured her that things would go well. Lynn had not spent a lot of time in the past, involved with activities with acquaintances in the class. For the past, several, years, Allison and Jean had been completing activities with Lynn.

When Allison and Lynn moved to the town three years ago, they met Jean.

Allison had given Jean a key to the home after Lynn continued to want to go next door to visit their neighbor. Jean watches Lynn, at the home she shares with Zealand. Jean had not wanted to leave Zealand by himself.

After, several, minutes, Allison recollected her thoughts, and read her messages. They were from prospective clients that had recently submitted for a loan.

Allison began making calls. The clients were grateful that Allison had done that. Allison told them, that she will need to obtain more information.

Mark had been working in real estate, several, years longer than Allison. They became acquaintances when she began working at Delkes Realty.

Allison awoke Lynn early that next morning. She reminded Lynn, that she had school. Allison wanted Lynn to be ready for the new activities that Lynn would have at school that day. They sat at a small breakfast table, and ate breakfast. Allison made tea, because she knew it was a favorite of Lynn.

Allison walked Lynn inside the classroom, and there had been other children sitting at their desks.

The teacher Ms. Rosner approached them.

"I have enjoyed being a grade school teacher. This is an important time for Lynn Randall. Lynn will reconnect with the other students. I have plenty of things prepared for the class today".

Ms. Rosner was pleasant.

Allison felt that her daughter's teacher was ready to spend time with the class.

Ms. Rosner asked Allison about her career.

Allison told the woman about the, several, years she spent assisting a gown designer, and that she enjoyed the business.

"I enjoy being creative. Designing gowns had been a lot of responsibility. I was working longer hours at home. The designer and I created many gowns that were original. Real Estate is also nice".

"The children are excited, to be in class. I do not blame them. I must have seen every parent today. After, several, years in this building, they are assigned to a different school".

Allison felt bad for leaving Lynn.

Her daughter waved to her, as Allison left the classroom.

When Allison returned to the office, Mark wanted to know the details of the first day of school for Lynn. Lately, Mark asked Allison the details of her life.

Allison briefly told Mark about the conversation that she had with Ms. Rosner. When they finished their conversation at the office, people were already leaving the office for the day.

Allison and Mark walked to their cars together.

Mark began to talk about his family.

Mark and Allison talked of, several, people that had not come to work. They had been used to it. The majority of the people at the office, at times chose to do their own activities during the day. The majority of the office had families. Everyone had their own, schedule. Some of the staff also had their own meetings throughout the day. The day sometimes went by fast.

Allison thought about the things, that she had to do the next day.

Jean and Lynn were outside. They were adding plants to the garden. Lynn finished the last of the gardening. She knew that it was time to go home.

Jean talked with Allison.

"Gardening was our activity today. I asked Lynn about school. Lynn mentioned that her teacher talked about gardening. I thought it would be nice if we added something to the garden".

"My days seem to go faster, since I have stopped traditionally working".

Before they left, Jean handed Allison some vegetables that were in the garden.

When Allison and Lynn arrived home, Allison prepared the vegetables.

Lynn decided to eat fruit, while she waited for dinner. Lynn reminded Allison, that Jean and she ate a snack two hours ago.

Allison was glad that her daughter was becoming self-sufficient.

After dinner, Allison assisted Lynn to prepare for school the next day. Lynn had a long day, and had not found it difficult to rest that evening.

Allison looked over some notes. Allison had rarely been able to complete her work at the office. Allison visited with numerous clients over the years about their loans.

Allison was at her desk that next day. Allison planned to complete most of her work, before she leaves the office.

Allison attempted to call a client that designed antique silverware. Recently, the client planned to create, several, designs, and take them to a distributor. They would often choose one design.

"I do not mind having their contract. I have been working with them for, several, months. I took my time on my latest design. I always enjoy thinking of new ideas".

"Do you know of anyone involved in this specific design work"?

Allison responded with a no.

"Every so often, I have meetings in places outside of town. This is why my time is limited today. I apologize if I made you change your schedule for today. In fact I' am supposed to ride a train out tomorrow. I enjoy the particular house that you showed me. I was hoping that we could take care of the details of the contract. The interest is something I would like to know about".

Allison had gone through the document. This was a normal routine for her. Allison explained several, points, in detail.

"If you were in my position Allison, would you take this particular house"?

The woman and Allison, had silence around them, as they sat at her desk. Allison and the woman looked to be close acquaintances. The woman signed the document for the house.

Things inside the office had become hectic. Allison asked Mark to come to her desk, several, times, to confirm information.

An hour before Allison was scheduled to leave, her phone rang.

Mark asked Allison to shut his office door, if it had not been closed.

"I will be gone for, several, days. My family, and I, will attend, a meeting with a business organization that my wife is a member of. There will be a banquet. Gillian had been with the organization for at least ten years. We are leaving in the morning. When we arrive at the end of the weekend, David will be prepared for school on Monday".

Allison talked of Lynn. She told him that Lynn was adjusting to her new class.

"I' am unsure of when Jean will stop staying with her".

Allison poured a cup of coffee that was inside the office. The coffee was primarily for the clients, but rarely did someone from the office bring coffee from home.

An hour later, Allison decided to go to a small restaurant that many people working in the area frequented. Allison ordered a coffee, and began reading through the newspaper. The restaurant had become over booked. Allison had not noticed anyone in particular. Allison had been reading, when a gentleman approached her.

"I had been watching you. I was wondering what you did as a career".

He remained silent for, several, seconds.

Allison told the gentleman, that she processed real estate loans.

"I would offer you a job to assist me with my work, but you may be too busy with real estate. Have you thought of taking a set of professional photos"?

Allison told the gentleman, that she had not. She told him about the gown boutique, where she worked with Sara.

"That must have been quite an experience to work with a designer. I decided to become a photographer. I graduated from the university. I worked for, several, years at a restaurant. An acquaintance, owned the business".

Allison remained quiet for, several, seconds.

She agreed to have photos taken of her.

"Then I guess it is settled. You will meet me here in the morning. Then we can visit my studio. Remember to be on time".

Allison had agreed, once again.

"I apologize that I have to leave at this time. I' am working on a photo shoot. I have been trying to take photos of the main city. The photo shoot has been taking me a while to complete. It has lasted nearly three months".

"I think that you should bring, several, pieces in your wardrobe with you. That way we could create a different look throughout the photo shoot".

Allison finished her coffee.

The gentleman waved to her as he walked out the restaurant door. Allison noticed the car that the gentleman had driven. He had been informative about photography. Allison never noticed the gentleman inside the restaurant before.

An hour later, Allison found Lynn inside drawing.

Lynn greeted Allison, and told her that she had to complete an arithmetic assignment. Lynn was calm, as if she had not wanted to make her assignment complicated.

"Before you arrived, Jean and I were talking about the city where she was born".

Lynn began to organize her things.

Moments later, Allison and Lynn were leaving the home.

Allison decided not to mention the photographer to Jean. She wanted to talk with her daughter, before she told Jean.

Allison and Lynn were sitting in the car. Allison mentioned that they would visit a boutique. She told her daughter about the gentleman inside the restaurant. Allison told Lynn about his career. The gentleman wanted to take photos of Allison. She told Lynn the professional photos would be taken at his studio.

Lynn was glad for Allison.

Allison and Lynn had gone inside the boutique, and found, several, pieces to add to Lynn's wardrobe.

Allison and Lynn arrived home.

Allison and Lynn decided to eat dinner on the outside patio. They enjoyed their time outside.

"Ms. Rosner told us today, that we would have a longer weekend this week".

Lynn began to talk about the class hamster.

"Within two weeks, Ms. Rosner said that the hamster had grown".

Allison listened to her daughter.

"I think Ms. Rosner may begin to give the class more assignments".

Allison told Lynn, that she would assist her with her assignments if she needed her to.

The sky had begun to darken. It had been noticeable not long before. Lynn continued to work inside. Allison found the newspaper.

Allison cleaned the kitchen, and reminded Lynn of the hour.

Lynn told Allison that she had a long day in class.

"I had a long day. I had a great time being around my classmates. We all began to socialize together".

Lynn had begun putting away her things. Lynn had not wanted her art supplies to become broken. Lynn finished.

It had been nearly ten in the evening. Within twenty minutes, Lynn had closed her eyes for the night.

Allison enjoyed being a parent.

Allison had this thought in her mind, as she went to the restaurant that day.

Lowell had arrived to the restaurant before her. He had been sitting next to a window with a cup of coffee in his hands. Lowell finished his coffee, when Allison approached him. He asked her about Lynn.

Allison told Lowell, that Lynn had been fine.

"You are going to have a great time modeling, and learning photography. I will take, several, photos. I have been doing photography for a while. I need you to be patient with me".

Lowell said this, as Allison and he walked toward his red sedan.

"Allison I own two cars. I drive them both. My red sedan reminds me of the summer".

Lowell and Allison drove to a house adjoining a marina. The house had been difficult to notice driving along the main road.

Lowell and Allison passed through, several, rooms, before they came upon where he wanted to bring her.

There had been a studio organized with, several, photo lamps.

"I organized this room to allow me to take many different kinds of photos".

Lowell had shown Allison, where there had been, several, backgrounds.

Allison found her suitcase, and selected something from her wardrobe.

"I have to say, that I' am not a clothes or gown designer. We can try different combinations with your wardrobe".

Lowell began taking photos.

"I want you to have, several, photos to bring home".

Before Lowell and Allison, had taken a break, he organized a room to develop the film.

Allison sat in a chair.

An hour had gone by, before Lowell and Allison finished the photo shoot.

"You did wonderful work Allison. I' am unsure of the length of time I will need to develop the film. As soon I finish developing the film, I will give you copies".

Lowell said this, as he began putting some of his equipment away.

Allison began to assist him.

Lowell drove Allison to the restaurant, where her car had been parked. Her car was a four door.

"We have arrived. Would you like to go inside the restaurant for a cup of coffee"?

Allison decided on a cup of tea instead.

"I have to say that your daughter is glad to have a mother such as you. I' am sure Lynn appreciates the time you spend with her. I decided to move into this part of town, several, years ago. I wanted to go to school for finance. There are, several, photographers, I have met over the years".

Lowell continued.

"Several, of them, I have remained close to over the years. At least I found something that I enjoy a lot. I think that my photography is the best thing for me. I have learned a lot. I have gone out of town a lot. I have painted, several, paintings. I have received, several, requests to have three of my paintings displayed. Allison, I' am sure that you have experiences with art. When I noticed you, I had not assumed what your career had been".

Allison explained that she spent a limited amount of time inside the office. Allison completed a lot of interviews about the loans that she processed, at other places.

"There are many things to do in modeling and photography".

Allison and Lowell had remained at the restaurant for a while. An hour later, they left. Lowell drove past the entrance, as Allison walked to her car.

As usual her daughter had been glad to see her.

"I told Ms. Anders about your day. That you were a model taking photos".

"I did not know that you were interested in photography or modeling. I heard it from Lynn. I asked her where the photographer lived. Lynn said that she had not known. Lynn knew a limited of information about him. Lynn knew that the photographer lived not far from here. I lived here for a while, but I have never met this photographer".

Jean smiled.

Jean had worn a simple brown cardigan that day.

"We had not completed any activities, the several, hours that you were gone. I think Lynn is slowly becoming used to a limited of time for other activities. Lynn does not have the whole day anymore, as in the past".

Allison asked Jean, if she would like to have a late lunch with Lynn and herself.

Jean reminded Allison, that she was expecting some acquaintances that afternoon. It would probably be best if she remained at home.

Allison told Jean, that she understood. Allison knew that they would do something at a later time. Allison knew that Jean had rarely made plans with her acquaintances.

Allison and Lynn walked home. They decided that evening, that they would eat their dinner outside. They had been enjoying eating outside lately. It had been a nice alternative. Allison decided that she would make a vegetable soup. It had not taken Allison and Lynn long to eat. When Allison is around her daughter, she feels, several, years younger.

That particular evening, Allison asked Lynn, if she could assist her with the dishes. They worked. They read the newspaper, and talked of the events. They were sitting inside the living room. They owned, several, furnishings.

The next day, Allison heard the phone ring. When Allison answered it, she realized that it had been Lowell.

"I hope that I' am not waking you. I wanted to inform you that I was able to develop the film. I was hoping that you would take a look at them. I will be able to give you copies".

Allison thought for a moment.

"I will make a phone call. Maybe my neighbor Jean is not doing anything, and will be able to keep Lynn company".

When Allison called Jean, Allison had given her some of the details about the previous day. Allison promised that she would arrive home in a short while.

Allison heard a knock at the door. Allison had been expecting Jean. Allison opened the door, and Jean had come inside. Allison explained to her, that Lynn had been sleeping.

Allison and Jean drank a cup of tea.

Allison drove to the home of Lowell.

Lowell answered his door, after Allison knocked once.

Allison followed behind Lowell, as he continued to walk through his home. They had gone into a different room.

"I created the photo, into an eight by ten".

Allison was glad of the transformation in the actual photo. Allison felt that Lowell had done a wonderful job. They continued to talk of the photos from the photo shoot.

Lowell and Allison looked through other images. He had been glad that his work turned out well.

"I do appreciate your patience. If at some time in the future, you would like for me to change the size of the photos, I would be able to do that for you".

Allison thanked him.

"I would like for us to work together more. I work with, several, different photographers. I think that over time, you will continue to learn modeling".

Lowell autographed the back of the photos.

"Would you want to complete some work during this upcoming week"?

Allison told Lowell, that she would need to call him, and give him the time, and date. She traveled in and out of the office often throughout the day.

Lowell asked Allison to take photos of things throughout the day.

Allison thought for a moment about the request of Lowell to take photos. After, several, seconds, Allison understood.

"Allison, I do think that we will work well together. Again, the important thing when taking photos is going through the process. Allison some of the photos I have seen of some of my colleagues have been well done. The ideas were great".

Lowell was sure that he wanted to work with Allison.

The closest Allison had come to learning about photography, was when she assisted Sara with her gown boutique. Since, Allison and Sara had spent a lot of time designing gowns they would attend events. Allison would often take photos. Allison enjoyed selling the gowns with Sara. She mentioned this to Lowell.

After their conversation, Allison had been fine with their most recent plans. They decided on their favorite photo. They choose a photo that had scenery in the background.

Early afternoon, Allison arrived home. Allison planned to show Lynn, the, several, copies of the photos she had brought home.

Allison and Lowell worked, throughout the week.

Allison promised Lowell, that they would meet later, that afternoon. It had been midmorning. Allison needed to make a call to the bank. The call would be regarding, one of the loans, she was trying to process.

By the time Allison finished the call, she had known, that she had a limited amount of time, to submit the documents. Allison had not known how long the call would take. Allison completed the first, several, forms.

After Allison went through the familiar routine with the documents, Allison had to meet Lowell, at a nearby restaurant.

When Allison arrived, Lowell had already arrived at the restaurant. He had been seated, and waiting for her. Lowell greeted Allison, as he kissed her cheek.

"I must say, it is a pleasure to be around you Allison".

The waitress brought them two cups of warmed tea.

Lowell and Allison sat across from one another. He began to talk about photos he had taken for recent clients. The models enjoyed their work. Some of the models had other careers.

"I' am hired once or twice, and I never hear from the clients, again. Maybe the reason is that some of the clients I work with would rather change the layout, of the photo shoot. Things sometimes are never the same, as a photographer. Allison, I know that modeling is new for you. As I mentioned, I will do my best, to assist you with your career. I' am sure that we can work together, as long as you remain, patient with me".

Lowell was being direct. Allison could remember Sara this way at times.

28

"I enjoy knowing the details of my work. I' am used to traveling. I do enjoy that. Twice, I completed a photo shoot for two separate magazines. When I finished working with the staff of the magazines, they told me that they would contact me in the future. There had been many interesting projects I have been part of. Many of the photo shoots I do continue to be well thought out. Of course, I have been successful with weddings. That is the synopsis of my career".

Allison felt that the things Lowell had done had been interesting. She understood how they could become part of his career. Allison thought that in some ways, Lowell had similar ideas as her.

The sky had been clear, and she drove to another studio. It had been a small room.

"I need to finish setting up the camera equipment. You should probably go ahead, and change your wardrobe piece. I have coffee that is made".

Allison began drinking a cup of coffee.

Allison wore a silver dress. Lowell took, several, photos. They finished with the first set of photos.

Allison wore a red dress, redone her hair, and added on heavier makeup.

"Allison, your makeup looks great".

Allison had not been thinking of anything specific during the photo shoot. Allison wanted to look prepared. Allison had gradually become less nervous.

"The photos are coming out well".

Lowell asked Allison, what she had been thinking of then.

Allison responded truthfully, when she told him real estate. It had taken them another hour to finish.

"Allison, I would want us to go sightseeing for areas I could use in future photo shoots. There are many locations in this town. We could visit, several, places".

Lowell stood beside Allison, and repositioned her stance. He began taking more photos.

"It must be bothersome, having long photo shoots".

Allison had looked at the time on a clock that had been in the room. Allison realized that it had been almost time for her meeting with a client. Allison had been thinking of the work at the office, while at the photo shoot. Her schedule at the real estate office would be hectic over the next, several, weeks. The office had more business over the summer months.

Allison drove the twenty miles in her car.

When Allison arrived, she had not seen the gentleman. They were meeting at a restaurant that Allison was unfamiliar with. Allison waited in front of the building for him.

The gentleman found Allison, after he finished parking his car.

After, several, moments the gentleman approached Allison. He informed her, about part of his day.

"I hope that you do not mind that we meet here. My meeting with an executive took longer than I thought. I' am a businessman. My wife suggested we buy another house in the city. We agreed upon a larger scale house. The loan we are unsure of. The bank had not minded assisting us in the past. That was when we decided to choose the real estate firm that you work for. I heard good things about Delkes Realty. You must have had other meetings today".

Allison told the gentleman, that this was her only meeting.

"Some people do not understand my busy schedule, except my wife. We were married last year. Do you have any children"?

"I do have one daughter".

"I' am taking photos with a photographer, by the name of Lowell. We have been working together for a while".

"I do not think I' am familiar with this gentleman".

Allison told him that he had been a photographer for many years, and attended the university in the city.

"I have numerous photographers taking my photo. I use the photos for work. There are magazines that ask me to write articles".

He continued to talk about the property for sale.

"The house that we want has, several, bedrooms. Even though we live alone, my wife and I realize we may not always be by ourselves".

The gentleman noticed the waiters that were walking around. He continued to watch them, until he noticed Allison asking him a question about the menu.

"I do think that would be best with the wine selection that we chose".

They had a glass of wine.

"I do not spend as much time out anymore, unless I' am meeting someone for a reason".

Allison told the gentleman, that she spent time at some of the boutiques in the town.

"That would be great for my wife".

He moved his glass aside.

"I think that, I have had about enough to drink. I had planned on drinking a glass of wine".

Allison mentioned more about her life.

Allison mentioned, to the gentleman, that Lynn enjoyed drawing.

Allison remained silent for the gentleman to talk.

"I apologize, that I have to close this meeting. I' am supposed to be out of the area for, several, days. I need to find out the details. I' am glad, that we were able to finalize the loan. I hope everything continues to go well with both your careers. I' am meeting with, several, executives tomorrow, and could recommend Delkes Realty".

The gentleman mentioned, that if he needed anything else, that he would call the real estate firm.

Allison drove to visit Lowell at his photo studio.

Allison told Lowell, about her earlier meeting.

"I' am grateful for the amount of work I receive".

Allison looked at, several, photos.

"Allison, I was preparing dinner. You are more than, welcome to join me".

Allison agreed.

Lowell and Allison sat at a table, in the middle of the room. They were silent for, several, moments, before they talked about the places he had visited with his career. Things had been going well for Lowell.

"I have had bad times, as well as good times, with my career Allison".

Lowell continued talking.

"I know that you enjoy reading the news. You are welcome to read the newspaper".

Lowell handed Allison, that day's newspaper.

Later, Allison realized the time.

"The skies are becoming dark. Lynn is waiting for me. She is spending time with our neighbor.

Allison left the home of Lowell.

Allison drove her car away.

Lowell is a good person. Allison appreciated the knowledge that he was giving her about modeling, and photography. Allison was interested, in traveling with her modeling career. Allison had not in the past, thought of traveling the way, that she had now.

Allison realized, that Jean, and Lynn, had arrived home moments ago.

"We had not heard from you, and decided to begin dinner. I thought that if you came home, before we finished, that you would be able to join us".

Allison decided to join, Jean, and Lynn. Before Jean left, she, and Allison cleared the dishes.

Lynn began to talk of the day she had with Jean.

"We spent the day talking about the city that Ms. Anders, was from. Ms. Anders told me, that she often talks with her family. That she wants me to come with her next time, she visits them. Ms. Anders promised me, that she would keep me informed, when she visits again. Ms. Anders has not given up on the idea, for us to come with her".

Allison had been glad, that her daughter was adjusting to living, with one parent.

"Earlier, I finished my assignment for class".

Lynn thought, that she needed rest.

"Maybe we can talk, more tomorrow".

Lynn was confident, that she would fall asleep quickly. Lynn had been trying to get more rest, since being in her new class.

Allison enjoyed being a mother. She assisted her daughter, where she could.

Allison had not known if she would, have another child.

At this time, Lynn had not minded being an only child. Lynn was adjusting to not having Edgar around her all the time. He remained involved, in an organization that assisted in promoting relief and peace. The group continues to travel.

Jean had become a great acquaintance. She mentioned that she had spent a lot of time doing activities with her family, when she was growing up. Jean enjoyed that routine with family.

Allison finished her warmed cup of tea, and decided to remain downstairs.

"We went to the park yesterday, Mark told Allison. David had come down the slide, and somehow managed, to twist his ankle. Gillian and I had to take him to the emergency room. We had to remain at the emergency room with David, for a while. The nurses assisted him to balance his walk. David is doing better. He will miss about a week of school. He began school, last Monday".

"David is an active child".

Allison remembered when David, was, several, months old.

"The family was supposed to go out for dinner. Instead, we stayed home, and prepared dinner".

Allison was not looking forward, to being put in the same situation. Allison had known that one day, Lynn would hurt herself.

Mark and Allison walked to the staff break room, where they were supposed to attend a staff meeting. It was supposed to last, for, several, minutes.

Allison walked toward her desk, with Mark beside her.

At the meeting, several, people asked questions about the procedures, that everyone was supposed to follow, before processing a loan application.

"We need a signature of Darrell, before we process the applications. I think sometimes, the procedures can be confusing. He gives the realtors updates to changes, and then they change again. We often have meetings, with the banks that we are in contact with".

Allison felt bad, that he was concerned about the changes.

"Gillian is staying at home with David, to keep him company. Gillian is visiting his school, for his assignments. I feel bad for him. He wants to be at school. Lately, he has been asking for toys. I do not blame him for wanting to keep entertained".

Allison glanced at the time. There had not been anything out of the ordinary in her routine that day. Allison talked with Lowell.

Lowell told Allison that he had been in town. He planned to go into the city, and wanted to meet with her.

"We could visit a restaurant. I know that you enjoy being in the city. I will show you the photos, when we get together".

Allison told Lowell that she needed to finish some work inside the office. Allison had a meeting. Then, Allison wanted to get home to Lynn.

"That is fine. I have other business that needs to be completed. I have to call back the newspaper. They wanted to complete an article with a photo that I had taken with my camera. I agreed to let them use the photo".

"While you get some work done, I will look into my work that needs to be completed".

The only routine to Allison's day was seeing Lynn after class.

Allison enjoyed spending time with Lowell. He was a good acquaintance. Lowell had known a lot about photography. Allison became worried that he would become annoyed with her lack of knowledge with photography. He had been patient with her. He was detail oriented with his work. Allison had always wanted to do something as interesting as modeling. A while later Allison left the office.

An hour later, Allison finished the meeting about the property.

Whenever Allison mentioned that she was once a real estate broker, people were confused. They were wondering why she decided to stop selling real estate. Allison told anyone that asked her, that she had often been gone away from home, for more than a day at a time. There had been things that Allison had to cancel. Allison felt bad for needing to be as dedicated to real estate.

Allison not too long ago, moved in order to accommodate her new lifestyle.

Allison began a call with a bank. She had to submit new information to them. Allison waited through an operator. She was finally transferred to a gentleman. Allison had never talked with him before.

Over the past, several, years processing loans, Allison managed to meet, and know many accountants.

Clint came on the line, and explained the procedures of the bank.

He had been able to finalize the loan. Clint told Allison that the client would need to complete the rest of the details with Delkes Realty.

Allison had been glad that the documents were able to be completed.

Clint reminded Allison, that if the office had any additional questions that they could contact the bank. They ended their conversation.

Allison thought back to their conversation, after she sat down the phone. Allison knew his work had been difficult.

Allison began driving home late afternoon. She thought of not wanting to begin another dating relationship at this time. Allison thought things were the way that they were meant to be.

Lynn walked toward Allison, as she heard the front door open. She had been at home by herself.

"Allison, do not worry. I arrived, several, moments ago. Ms. Anders decided to let me walk home alone. She said that you called her, several, minutes, before you left your meeting, and told her that you were on your way home. I hope that you are not disappointed".

An hour later, Allison and Lynn were sitting at the table, and eating their dinner.

Lynn began to tell Allison that there had been a young gentleman in the class that seemed to get into trouble every day.

"Today he tried to feed the class pet some of his lunch. He had been told that he would have to remain inside the classroom throughout the class break. He had not liked that".

Lynn asked Allison about the children in the class growing up.

Allison told Lynn, that there had been children that sometimes had not followed instructions.

"Allison, I will continue to keep you informed if anything else happens. I' am sure that Jacob will continue to get in trouble, until he listens to the teacher. My teacher, Ms. Rosner is married, and said that she has a teenage daughter. Maybe we can invite them to our home. We could play board games. That is one of my favorite things to do. I do draw, most of the time".

Lynn smiled.

"I think it would be nice to have another sibling. It would be interesting to see how they are able to play board games. I' am sure I will eventually have acquaintances in my class. During the day we take an hour break at school. We eat lunch, and then have free time".

The phone had begun ringing. It was Lowell calling.

"Allison, we must have both had a busy day".

Allison explained a meeting that she had earlier that day.

"I understand now. Things are never, tiring, for us. I had visited, two towns, the past, several, days. I wanted to see if any offices needed any photographers. They told me that they would contact me if they had any work. It would not be for another several weeks. When I visited some photographers I knew in the area, we spent time sharing ideas. That is one way, that we remain updated about photography. I cannot remember a time when any of us had not done photography".

It was obvious that Lowell enjoyed his work.

"I recently have shown other photographers my work, and they liked it. Promise me that you will meet me tomorrow. I have collected some photos of some of my colleagues, and could show you. There is one photo that shows a gorgeous sunset. He had to wait for three hours, before he was able to take a photo of the scene. Allison I know that you are more interested in modeling than photography".

Allison continued to listen as Lowell discussed his experience at the event.

"A woman approached me, and told me that she had seen an exhibit inside of a studio located in the city. It was designed by a local artist by the name of Swenson. He has been completing photography for, several, years. Swenson began his career at a later age".

"The woman wondered if I had ever heard of the art of Swenson. I told her that I had never seen the studio. I told the woman, that I had been visiting from out of town".

Lowell told Allison that he had planned to visit again. He wanted her to come with him. Allison had agreed that it would be a nice idea. She would have to make sure that she did not schedule any meetings. Maybe Allison would go into the office, later than her usual time.

Allison had planned to spend the next morning with Lynn.

Allison had been startled awake by a noise. Seconds later, she completely had awoken.

Allison had come downstairs.

Lynn had been reading the newspaper.

Allison had been glad to see her daughter.

"I know that you read the news. There was an accident that occurred on the highway".

Allison and Lynn ate breakfast.

After breakfast, Lynn decided to draw.

Allison felt that three hours went quickly.

Later, Allison and Lynn visited, several, clothing boutiques that were in close proximity. Allison wanted to buy Lynn additional pieces for her school wardrobe.

Allison had been at the studio of Lowell. They were looking over the photos that he recently had taken. In the photos Lowell had taken, the models were used, to the camera. They all wore different designs.

Lowell began critiquing his work. He had taken out his camera.

Allison had been wearing her wardrobe piece for the photo shoot.

Allison had, several, pieces in her wardrobe. She chose a cream suit that she had out of the five that were hanging. Allison had worn a cream scarf that she thought would match the suit. It had been left at the studio. The scarf was used for a previous photo shoot. She had seen it, several, times, but had not had a chance to wear it.

Lowell mentioned to Allison, that she looked, as if she were thinking, of other things.

Allison told Lowell, that she had things that she had to complete inside the office.

Allison focused her attention on the photo shoot. She had not thought that the photo shoot would take as long.

By the time the photo shoot ended, it had been time for Allison to leave. She needed to return to the office. Allison had forgotten the documents of one of the clients on her desk. She needed to complete some work on the file at home.

When Allison arrived to the office, Ophelia had been the last person there. She had been holding a phone conversation. Ophelia had a real estate practice book in front of her. She noticed Allison.

"One of our clients is upset. He said that he does not want to purchase the house. The client claims that the house has things that may go wrong. He claims that he did not have any issues when he bought the house, that he is living in currently".

Ophelia continued to listen to the client.

"He has a right to want the issues stated in the contract. I explained that sometimes it is difficult to know everything that may go wrong. I hope that he agrees to have the house reexamined by someone else. I think that it will assist him to understand more about the house. I' am unsure of how to handle this issue".

Ophelia tried to smile, in hopes of feeling better about the situation.

The office had dealt with unsatisfied clients in the past. The office tries to stay in communication with clients.

"That is why I try to have the agent remind them about any potential adjustments to the house, before their loan is processed. They receive a lot of background information".

Ophelia turned away from Allison as she listened to the gentleman on the phone.

Allison had not encountered the particular situation. She felt bad for Ophelia.

Allison made a call to the prospective client. She explained her schedule, and he seemed to understand. He mentioned that he had also been running late.

Allison found the restaurant. There had been, several, cars in the parking lot. It continued to remain that way.

"I wanted to meet here, because it is close to my office. I have a limited amount of time today".

As the gentleman and Allison were seated, he asked Allison where she lived. He thought he recognized her.

Allison told the gentleman, that she lived not far from the town most of her life.

He refocused on the meeting.

"I enjoy working with Delkes Realty. The firm sold me the home that I' am moving from. We are deciding to sell it, because my wife and I needed to move her parents with us. We thought that we should have more space for them. They have accumulated a lot of things over the years".

The gentleman understood the business of real estate. The gentleman and Allison waited until after they ordered a glass of water, before they continued their conversation.

"The process, with our loan, has been long. I' am unsure if it has anything to do with the sell of our current home. Things are busy for us now. My wife is visiting doctors about her parents' health. Things happen, as we become older. The staff at the facility they were at had been great in assisting us with the process to bring them home. My wife felt bad, when we initially decided to let them stay at the facility. She wanted her parents to live with us a while ago".

The gentleman asked Allison about her life.

Allison mentioned that she enjoyed completing gown designs for a number of years. She mentioned the time she spent designing gowns in the past. Allison told the gentleman, she later, began selling real estate.

The gentleman continued to talk about his family. He told Allison about the length of time he had been married.

"Our wedding had been with about a hundred guests. It lasted for, several, hours. Our family spent time with us. We decided to host the wedding over the weekend. My wife and I spent time, carefully planning the event. I had not known that there would be as many details as there had been".

The gentleman explained to Allison about his knowledge of the real estate contract. He continued to talk, while he signed his loan documents.

"Allison, I' am sure there will come a time that we will come across one another again".

The gentleman had shaken Allison's hand, and finished his glass of water.

Allison had gotten inside her car. As she closed her door, it began to rain. The roads were slick, but she continued to drive until she reached the office.

Once Allison reached the office, the rain stopped. Allison had, several, messages on her desk. Allison needed to return some calls.

Allison waited at the office a while longer.

Allison was preparing to leave, when the main door opened, and startled her.

It had been a woman wanting assistance with a new house.

"I plan to sell my current home. I plan to sell it, within, several, months".

The woman waited for Allison to assist her.

"I could give you the documents that you need to complete. You could take them home with you. Then, return them to the office, within, several, days".

Allison knew that the woman would return the completed documents to the office.

"I assume that your realtor will also assist me to choose a house. I do have one in mind. It is not far from my current home".

Allison noticed that the woman was beginning to become persistent at wanting things completed that evening. She assisted the woman, as best she could.

"My husband will provide most of the information. I worked a short time, when we were first married. We have been at our home, since after the fifth year that we were married".

The woman left, several, moments later.

Allison prepared to leave the office. She had a briefcase, and turned off the lights to the office.

Since a month ago, Allison had not heard of any criminal incidents in the area of the office. She hoped things would become normal near the office building. She continued to remain cautious.

Allison remained cautious as she drove away from the building. As she drove home, she thought of her daughter. They enjoyed their times together. Lately, their favorite thing to do was to eat outside, when it was warmer.

Allison had come home to a quiet home. She sat her briefcase down. She wore something different from her wardrobe. Allison knew Lynn was with Jean.

"You came in time. Lynn and I had a great time today. Lynn has been drawing. I had been preparing dinner. We were unsure of when you were coming home".

Allison, Lynn, and Jean were at the home of Jean.

"My day was long. I met with two clients. I had taken more photos with Lowell. I' am unsure of when he will develop the film. The photos will be part of an advertisement".

The photo shoot had been a long process. Allison had known that there were many details involved.

"Allison, I' am glad for you. You are beginning to enjoy your new career. I know that you will have success with it".

Allison and Jean raised their glasses. They had been having a great time that evening.

Lynn had begun, to look, older to Allison. Lately, she had not reminded Allison that she wanted to invite acquaintances over for dinner.

Lynn began to talk about the new pet the teacher brought to the classroom. It had been another hamster.

"Ms. Rosner told us, that it will live for a while".

Allison had been glad, that Lynn had been enjoying school. She would remember the time she is spending, with her classmates. Allison could hear Zealand barking outside. He was following, the birds.

Zealand walked into the home moments later, and began to wander around the dining room. He stopped. He had become still.

"I apologize to the both of you, but Zealand is enjoying himself. He is happy to be around all of us".

Jean called him, and he sat down beside her.

Jean excused them, and had begun to prepare dinner for Zealand.

"Zealand wants to eat with us. We should let him".

Zealand had been content. He remained, concentrating on eating.

Everyone finished eating. Zealand sat quietly watching them.

Lynn starred at Zealand, and he propped his head up. She ruffled him, and he, wanted to go outside.

An hour later, Allison, and Lynn walked home.

Allison and Lynn drank a cup of tea.

Lynn decided that she would rest.

Allison had come to check on Lynn, a while later. Lynn had already fallen asleep.

Allison had finished cleaning the kitchen.

Allison had been glad to hear from Lowell.

Lowell reminded Allison about the schedule he had that day.

"I received a call from an associate. He has been a photographer, longer than I. He invited me on a photo shoot with him. I will be gone for, several, days, and wanted you to know".

He provided Allison the number to the studio that they would be using.

"It will take me, several, hours to arrive there".

Allison thought the photo shoot would be great for Lowell.

The next morning, Allison parked on the other side of the building. She had been ready to begin her day.

Allison began walking toward the building.

Mark had gotten out of his car.

"I have some great news! Gillian found that she is pregnant again. She found out, after she became warm at work. She had gone home for a while. She never called me at work. After things had not changed, she went to the doctor".

"When I arrived to his office, the doctor told us that Gillian was pregnant. I think Gillian is hoping to have a girl. Needless to say, she is pregnant. We are becoming used to the news. She is about a month pregnant. The doctor told us that we would be fine. We were already familiar with pregnancy. We will need to buy, several, things for the baby".

Allison congratulated Mark on the pregnancy.

Mark asked Allison if she had any appointments that day.

Allison told Mark that she had.

Mark had been glad for the office. He told Allison this often, when she was able to process, several, loans in one week.

"We work hard at what we do Allison".

Allison was on a phone conference. She could hear her colleagues on their phones. They were probably arranging property showings.

Allison learned about, several, of the clients that she had to contact about properties.

The last meeting that Allison had with Mr. Emerald, had been over the phone. She had already had the documents prepared for the client.

Allison will wait for Sue Anne to bring her the documents she needed in order to complete the loan for the client.

Allison waited until midafternoon, before she left the office. She wanted to walk along an area of store fronts. There had been, several, clothing boutiques that Allison wanted to visit.

The boutique that Allison had been inside, sold clothing pieces for children. She spent, several, minutes looking around. Allison bought a newborn suit for the baby of Mark and Gillian. She planned to give it to Mark the following day. Allison knew that Mark planned to leave the office, by the time she returned.

The secretary had been at the office. She had an expression on her face, as if something, were bothering her. Mary answered the, several, calls that had come into the office.

Allison had been completing some work, and looking over, several, files. She had to leave for a meeting in, several, hours with Lilia Bell. Ophelia had decided to become an agent for the woman.

Lilia Bell called Allison earlier that day. She wanted to reconfirm the time of their meeting. Allison decided not to call Lilia. Instead she would drive to the home, and hoped that she would be there. They needed to talk about the details of her house.

Allison had been looking through files, when there had been someone holding on the line to talk with her.

Allison heard Lowell on the other end.

"I did not intend to take you away from your work. I did not think that you would mind if I called you at the office. Hopefully soon, we will be able to get your next modeling opportunity. I arrived into town yesterday".

"I had a photo of you. I was asked about your background as a model. An agency is doing an advertisement for a gown designer. The designer wants to bring more business to their designs. I told him that I would ask you, and then let them know".

She told him that she thought that it would be a good idea.

"I do think that this advertisement will be a great opportunity for you. It is something different, and I think that you would have a great time being part of it".

Lowell had been kind, and wanted Allison to understand the details for the advertisement. He had been helpful. Allison learned more about modeling, than she had in the past.

When Allison ended her telephone conference with Lowell, she walked toward the entrance where Mary sat.

Allison waited a moment, and then asked Mary how she had been doing. She had not wanted to pry into her personal life, but she was unsure of the reason something was bothering her.

When Mary began talking, she told Allison about the ended relationship with the gentleman she had been dating. They had been dating for, several, years. Mary and the gentleman had been living together. She recently moved in with an acquaintance that was going through a similar situation.

Allison told Mary that she felt bad for her situation.

"I am sure that one day things will change for you. You need to give it time".

Allison glanced outside, and noticed the sun was beginning to set.

Mary continued to explain that she had been volunteering for a local charity. She recently completed, several, local events.

"We thought that it would be best to end our relationship".

Allison had not wanted to be late to the meeting, but she mentioned Edgar.

"We do have Lynn. Edgar is involved in a peace organization. It is what he chose to do. He stays in contact with Lynn".

Allison handed the woman a cup of tea, and decided that in case traffic was congested at the time, that she should leave to the meeting. She knew that the secretary would be fine by herself. Allison left after their conversation. The traffic had been steady.

Allison arrived to meet with Lilia Bell.

"I was in the middle of preparing for our move. We had, several, people that have come to take a look at the things that we are moving. I' am unsure of when our move will be finalized".

Lilia offered Allison a cup of coffee. They sat down on a small deck. Lilia had been glad, that her husband and she were able to finalize, on another house.

"I' am glad that we have been here since our fifth year of marriage. Our daughter thinks that it is crazy that we would want to move now. We have been living in the home for a long time. When we bought our home, we went to the bank, and signed an agreement to purchase it".

An hour later, Lilia had taken Allison through a tour. It looked similar to the house next door. She had been glad, that her husband had been able to complete the documents.

"I apologize, if I caught you off guard the other day, at your office. Everything has been moving quickly for us".

Lilia thanked Allison, for the documents.

After she met with Lilia, Allison went to visit with Lynn. She had not needed to return to the office. Everyone would have left for the day.

Jean had been inside rearranging the kitchen.

"I bought some new things, to redo the kitchen. I thought, since I spent time in the kitchen, that I could at least redo my walls. I would have hired someone to assist me, but I thought that I could use my creativity, and redo the kitchen, on my own. I wanted to use a cream color".

"The idea has been, nice, so far, in my head. I have to say, I began the work sooner, than I thought. I have had the same design in my kitchen, for at least, several, years".

Allison had gone home.

Lynn arrived home.

"Allison, I enjoy my class. One day, I will imagine that I will have acquaintances".

She had begun sneezing, from the dog hair.

The fall weather had already begun. The first, several, years at school, were different for the students. The parents were required to provide the transportation, for their child. Most parents had chosen to bring their child to and from school.

Allison had not met any of the other parents.

Lynn had begun penciling on a drawing pad. She had not had any assignment, to complete that night.

While Lynn continued to draw, Allison read the news in the newspaper. There were stories of the events in the town. There had been a story on the funding of the local schools. Lynn continued to attend the local school.

Lynn had been sitting on the chair next to Allison. She had pencils that were sprawled out.

Things had been similar, that next day. Allison gave the gift for the baby to Mark.

He admired the design.

Mark told Allison, that he would bring the gift home.

Allison received, several, calls earlier, that day. At the next opportunity, Allison decided to call Sara. She heard her voice.

"Allison, I had not talked with you in a while. I sold, several, gowns, to several boutiques. A local magazine has told one boutique, to select one gown to go into their next issue. I will not know if they will select one of my gowns, until later. The staff informed me, that they would call".

Allison congratulated Sara.

"I' am sure, that they will decide to use one, of your gowns".

Allison and Sara talked for an hour about, the things that Sara had been doing with her design business.

Allison mentioned her career in modeling. Sara had not known, that Allison decided on the career of modeling.

"I know that you will do the things that you want with modeling".

"I have become even busier lately. I have been talking with more clients".

Allison had been glad to be able to talk, with Sara. She had been busier with work, since Allison stopped working for her.

Lately, Allison had been thinking of Lynn, and her, own career.

Mary walked toward Allison, with a bouquet of flowers.

"These are for you".

Mary handed them to Allison.

Allison opened the card, and noticed it was from Lowell. She thought it was nice of him, to send flowers to her work. She read the note, and realized, that it was reminding her of their dinner, that evening.

Allison remained on the phone with Sara. She mentioned to her, what happened. Allison began to tell Sara, about Lowell. She told Sara, about his background in photography. Sara thought that it was interesting. Lowell had been able to work, with many clients.

"Allison, if you want to wear one of my gowns anytime soon, then I will make sure, that I send it to you. I assume that your dress size has not changed. I recently designed, a gown that I know, you will like".

Allison and Sara ended their conversation.

Things were quiet at the office. Allison realized that everyone, else had gone home. She found, several, files that she needed, before she left out the door. She locked the door behind her.

Allison found the restaurant that Lowell and she had been to in the past.

"I ordered coffee. We can have dinner, after we leave here. I have an event that I have to attend, as part of a promotion, for a magazine. I hope that you will come. It will be, for, several, hours. I know, that you will not mind, being at the event".

Allison thought for a moment, before agreeing.

"Allison, I do think, that you will meet, a lot of nice people. They may have you assist them, with future modeling for them".

Allison waited for Lowell to finish his coffee. She wore the same clothes she had worn at the office. Lowell wore a black business suit.

Lowell drove Allison and him, to a restaurant that had been located, several, miles away.

As they entered the restaurant, Lowell mentioned, that he noticed someone familiar to him. The restaurant was dimmed. It had taken Allison, several, minutes, to become used to the lighting.

An hour later, Lowell and Allison, had not left the restaurant. By this time, they had been talking about photography. Lowell and Allison talked about the different techniques with photography.

"By the time, that you meet more individuals in the profession, then your career will be easier for you. They could assist you, with ideas involving modeling".

The waiter approached Lowell, and Allison.

Allison ordered a glass of water.

"Allison, we have been out for a while this evening. You have not even had a chance, to see Lynn ".

Allison agreed.

When Allison arrived to the home of Jean, she would bring Lynn home. Lynn would be restless. It was close to ten thirty that evening. She felt bad for keeping Lynn up past her bedtime. She had not had school the next day. Lynn was adjusting to having off two days out of the week.

Allison was in the newly redone kitchen. Jean was exhausted from a long day of remodeling the kitchen.

Allison and Lynn walked home. They were both exhausted from their long day.

Allison waited until later, to look at the photos Lowell had taken.

Lowell met Allison outside the office. She had gotten inside his car.

"We can come back for your car in, several, hours. I want you to be able to go home, and wear a different wardrobe piece, so we will not be late. Have you heard of any other incidents in this area"?

Allison told him that she had not.

"I hope that your car will be fine parked here".

Lowell and Allison both had gone inside the home. Lowell waited in the dining room for Allison. Lynn had been next door with Jean.

As they left the home, Lowell mentioned that Lynn may think that they were dating.

"We have become good acquaintances".

Lowell began to explain to Allison the kind of things to expect as they approached outside the event. She listened diligently as they walked inside.

There had been people socializing, and photos placed throughout the walls. Allison had been glad that she decided to come.

Allison went to the washroom, and wanted to reapply the makeup she had been wearing. She hoped the evening would go well. She knew that she would meet some skilled people.

When Allison left the washroom, she found Lowell, and stood next to him. He had a camera around his neck.

Allison followed Lowell, as he showed her, several, photos by people he had known.

Allison enjoyed the looks of one in particular that showed two horses galloping through a field. The sun had been out, and they were on a grassy hill side.

An hour later, the guests at the event had been talkative, after a long day of work. They remained patient throughout the event. Allison had taken a glass of wine that was offered to her. There were people that remained by themselves.

Allison watched as Lowell talked with, several, photographers he had known. He was used to this sort of event. Allison continued to enjoy her time that evening. Lowell exchanged contact information, with photographers, that lived in other places, outside the city. Everyone was glad, that things had been going well, that evening.

"Allison, it is nice to be around people that have similar interests, as you".

No one wanted to leave the event. There were two guest speakers. They talked about their work as photographers. They talked about the experiences, they had with their careers.

At eight that evening, things were similar to when, Lowell and Allison arrived. When she noticed similar photos again, Allison had been prepared to leave.

Lowell and Allison stopped, for coffee on the way home.

Allison had talked, with, several, photographers, at the event. She reminded Lowell, that she could understand why he enjoyed photography.

When Allison arrived home, Lynn had been expecting her.

Lynn asked Allison about the event.

Allison told Lynn about, several, of her favorite photos. She told her, that she would remember the event.

Allison knew that Lowell would call her that next day, at the office. They had become close acquaintances.

Lowell called Allison that next day, before she left for the office. He wanted to meet with her for coffee.

Allison agreed.

Lowell mentioned about a photo shoot he had completed the day prior. He had gone to a garden, and taken photos of some of the arrangements. Lowell told Allison, that it was a nice photo shoot. He was able to do something that he enjoyed.

"I' am excited to develop the film! I will show you the photos, when I' am finished".

Allison nodded in agreement.

"Allison, to remind you, I did mention you to, several, of the representatives yesterday. They would like to work with you sometime in the future".

Allison thought that was great news.

Allison noticed that everyone had been at the office.

Mark had come to the desk of Allison, after she finished her conversation.

"Allison, yesterday there was a gentleman that was in trouble. I' am unsure of all the details. I know that he had been walking to his car, and he suddenly had a difficult time breathing. Someone had been trying to assist him".

That morning Allison had gone inside the office later than her regular time. She continued to follow her regular schedule. Allison wanted to get some work done. She had not been to the office, since last week. Allison had, several, messages. She received two phone calls, before the end of the morning. She made, several, calls in order to respond back to the messages. After the phone calls, Allison left the office.

When Allison returned to the office, several, colleagues were talking about the gentleman that had been rushed to the emergency room. The gentleman worked, for a local company in the area. He had been spending time, with colleagues earlier, that evening.

It was difficult to know all the details. The police had not needed to complete an investigation. He was fine. The gentleman remained, at the local hospital.

Allison realized her desk phone had been ringing.

When Allison answered the phone, Jean had been on the other line. She explained that there had been a mechanical issue at Lynn's school. The school, decided to send the students home. Jean decided to pick Lynn up from school. Allison would not have to leave the office.

"I hope that is fine, with you. Lynn enjoys Zealand a lot. They are wandering around in the back of the house. I will let Lynn know, that we talked. She had been concerned about you today. I think the issue, at her school worried her. Lynn wanted to make sure, that you were alright".

They remained with their conversation, for, several, minutes. Allison had been glad, that Jean picked Lynn up from school.

Allison focused on the things that she had to complete, inside the office.

Allison promised Lowell, that they would have dinner together, that evening. They were supposed to meet at a restaurant in the city. It would take Allison, at least an hour and a half to drive. She planned to leave directly from work.

Allison felt bad, because this is one of the, several, times recently, that she could remember not eating dinner, with Lynn.

Allison had been glad, for the acquaintance that Lowell provided.

Allison walked inside the restaurant, and noticed, that Lowell had been wearing a sweater, and beige pants.

"Allison, I hope that this restaurant is fine with you. I was working today, and I finished, about an hour, before I came here. At first, I thought that I might be late. I thought it may be better, to meet at a restaurant in the city".

"I had a long photo shoot in the city. I met with a gentleman from an agency. He said that he needed some photos that his agency is supposed to give to a magazine. I' am unsure of what the magazine intends to do with the photos from the photo shoot. I' am sure, that the agency will use, several, of the photos. I mentioned to the gentleman that I was supposed to meet you here. That is why I decided to leave directly after the photo shoot".

Lowell and Allison talked about their careers. Lowell reminded Allison that he submitted some of the work they had done. It would take a while for the details to be put together for the advertisement.

Allison listened to Lowell. She thought that it had been great that they were interested in similar careers. Allison felt that she had to learn more about modeling.

Allison noticed the people around them, and stopped listening to Lowell for a moment. After a moment, she could understand the last of what he had been saying. Lowell mentioned inviting Lynn to dinner in the future.

Allison agreed that it would be a great idea.

"Lowell, I do think that she would enjoy that".

Lowell and Allison left the restaurant.

The kitchen smelled of the dinner that had been prepared that night. Jean and Lynn had dinner earlier. Allison realized that they must have eaten outside. When the cold weather began, it would remain for a while.

Allison read the messages that were on the table.

Allison found clothes that were inside boutique bags, on the table. There had been clothing for Lynn. Allison realized that Jean and Lynn had gone shopping. The school had gone at regular schedule that day. Jean and Lynn had been looking for something to do with their afternoon. Allison admired the designs of the clothing.

Allison prepared breakfast for Lynn and her, that next morning. Lynn came downstairs to the kitchen.

Allison and Lynn sat at the table in the kitchen.

Lynn began to tell Allison about her late afternoon adventures of buying, several, wardrobe pieces, with Jean the day before.

"Ms. Anders had not wanted me to become bored yesterday afternoon. She decided to drive us to the boutique to buy pieces for my wardrobe. An hour later, we were inside of a boutique".

Lynn had given Allison the updated information on her acquaintances at school.

"We thought that it would be nice to do an activity together outside of class".

She continued to talk about Ms. Rosner, and the rules that she had given the class.

Jean called, before Allison and Lynn finished their breakfast. She wanted to remind Allison about the clothes that she bought for Lynn. Jean hoped that Allison would not mind. She told her, that they had been gone for nearly an hour.

Jean waited for, several, minutes, before she asked Allison about her photo shoot that she had scheduled. It was supposed to be, later that day.

Allison told Jean that she thought the photo shoot would go well. She would have, several, photos taken of her, from a previous photo shoot she had done. Allison planned to wear, several, pieces from her wardrobe. She told Jean, that in the photo shoot she was going to wear a suit.

Allison enjoyed being a model. It meant a lot to her. Initially, she did not think that she would understand modeling. Lowell mentioned to Allison in the past, that models had a difficult time at some photo shoots.

Allison told Lynn about some of her photo shoots. Allison had not explained the difficulties of modeling to Lynn.

Jean had not known much about photo shoots. She never modeled before.

Jean asked Allison if she thought that Lynn would want to model when she became older.

Allison told Jean, that Lynn often asked her questions about modeling. She was unsure about Lynn's future plans.

Allison knew that Lynn would soon want to spend more time with her acquaintances.

Jean enjoyed being around Lynn, as she grew up.

Allison looked at Lynn. She was content at drawing. It was one of her favorite things to do.

After Allison ended the phone conversation, Allison and Lynn finished their breakfast.

Allison had not bothered Lynn, while she kept herself busy drawing. She finished, and decided to take a small break. Lynn had shown Allison the drawing.

Later that evening, Allison found the photos that she had. She brought them over to show her daughter. She had begun to intently look at the photos. Lynn had rarely seen Allison wear makeup. Lynn told Allison that she had done a great job. Lynn had known about the photos that Allison had been taking with Lowell.

"Would you like to come to dinner with us? Lowell has been asking about you recently. He thinks you may have a great time. You are able to come tomorrow evening if you want. School will be the next day, but we will not be long".

Allison phoned Lowell, and told him about her plans for them to have dinner with Lynn.

"This is fine for me, because we do not have any important business to discuss at this time. I have two appointments tomorrow. Two agencies plan to talk with me, to see if I would be willing to work with them".

Lowell had known the individuals with the agencies from working in photography.

"I do enjoy working with new people. They share new ideas from the previous work they had completed. Every photo shoot is a new experience".

Lowell understood the constant change he experienced as a photographer.

Lowell knew that Allison had a busy schedule. He knew that she had to constantly balance her work schedule, and spending time with Lynn. Lowell knew that Allison had become used to her rigorous lifestyle.

Allison mentioned to Lowell, that Lynn, several, years ago fell off of her bicycle, and had gotten right back on. She reminded him that now Lynn was able to balance herself when she rode her bike. Allison told Lowell that was something she tried to remember in her daily routine. Allison tried to always get back up when she had a difficult situation.

"Allison, I think that you do a wonderful job being a mother".

They ended their conversation. Allison appreciated the complement that Lowell had given her.

Lowell had been someone that Allison could talk with easily. Lynn was glad that Allison was working hard with her career as a model.

Allison waited a while, before she told Lowell that she should go. He understood, and wanted to develop film. Lowell confirmed where they would meet, and that he would see Allison the next day.

After Allison and Lynn ate breakfast, Lynn went next door to visit with Jean, and Zealand. Lynn played Frisbee with Zealand.

Allison had not planned to leave home, that morning. She wanted to remain home, in case Lowell called her for any reason. She had been looking forward to the dinner, that evening. Allison was glad, that Lowell invited Lynn, and her.

When Lowell, Allison, and Lynn arrived at the restaurant, there had been paintings surrounding the walls.

Lowell mentioned that he had been to the restaurant, several, times, in the past.

"Allison, you are one of my favorite people, to work with".

Lynn enjoyed being at the restaurant. Lowell asked Lynn about school and the acquaintances, that she has met.

There were, several, groups, at the restaurant.

Lowell and Lynn talked longer.

Allison watched them, as they talked. Since the restaurant had been in the city, Allison had not recognized anyone. As many times as she had visited into the city, she had never noticed the restaurant. She had gone many places around the city in the past, because of her real estate career.

Allison began listening to the conversation, between Lowell, and Lynn. She waited a while for them to finish. They had been talking about photography. Lynn told Lowell, that one day it would be nice to take photos. She had not had a camera, or had taken photos before. Lynn told Lowell, that she would have to ask Allison first.

Lynn drank the tea that she ordered. She noticed the atmosphere inside the restaurant.

"Allison, Lynn is talkative. She is knowledgeable on what is around her".

Lynn was having a great time at the restaurant.

"Allison, I decided to bring these photos, with me. They are previous photos I have taken in the past. This may help you to have more insight, into my career. It may assist you with ideas, on how you want to complete, upcoming photo shoots".

Allison agreed that it would assist her, as she looked through the photos.

Lowell, Allison, and Lynn had been surrounding the table an hour later. They finished eating.

Lowell and Allison talked about real estate. Lowell had not known as much about selling houses, as Allison. He recently talked with an acquaintance that wanted to buy another house.

"The process has been difficult for him. He has a busy schedule, and found it difficult, to make time, to contact local realtors about, the sell, of his home".

Allison provided Lowell the number to Mark. She told him, that he could assist the other photographer, with the, sell of his home.

Lowell told Allison, that the photographer would appreciate assistance, selling his home.

"I will call Daniel, with this information, in, several, hours. I' am sure, that he is going to want to contact Mark".

After, several, moments, Lowell, and Allison stopped talking.

Allison looked at Lynn, and could tell, that she had a long day.

"I think that we have been at the restaurant, long enough. My daughter is beginning to look, as if she had a long day".

Allison, Lowell, and Lynn walked out toward the car, and the ground had been wet from the previous rain. They had not, noticed the puddles.

They arrived home, and Lynn decided to fall asleep in her room. It had been late, and Allison would let Lynn continue to rest for the remaining of the night. Lynn would need her rest for school that next day.

Allison decided to go to bed shortly after.

When Allison brought Lynn to school, there had been, several, parents, walking with their students.

Allison assured Lynn, that she would be fine by herself.

Lynn walked inside the building by herself.

Allison remembered when her mother had taken her to school. They would often walk inside the school building together.

When Allison had arrived inside the office, things had been their usual. Several, of her colleagues, and been on the phone. They would most likely remain that way for a while.

Darrell mentioned that there would be a brief morning meeting. The meeting would be an update to the changes in the contract. The lawyer had a meeting with him, and showed him the area in the contract that needed to be updated. One of the most important things would be to know the amount of percentage of interest in the contract. The meeting had ended after, several, minutes. The manger had another meeting that he had to attend at another office.

After the meeting, everyone went back to finish their work. Darrell watched everyone return back to what they were doing.

Mark remained at his desk. He had, several, clients that he was assisting. Mark had been trying to complete some work. He had been on the phone for a while.

It was an hour, before Allison completed her last call. There was a potential for a new client. The gentleman assured Allison, that he would decide to come to the office within, several, days. There had been a house that the gentleman had been trying to sell. He had been living there for, several, years.

Allison told the gentleman that she would verify the amount of interest on the loan. She would put together the documents, and then give him a call back. Completing the contract had been difficult at first. She had not known all the information. From what she remembered he explained that his previous spouse had been a kind and patient person.

"She moved into her own home a while ago. We have two dogs that we were taking care of for, several, years. They are older, but move around easily".

"We decided, they would live, with me".

Allison finished the conversation, with the gentleman. Before Allison sat the phone in the cradle, the gentleman agreed to meet Allison, at the office the next day. He had, several, addresses in mind of places he wanted to move to. When they ended their conversation, she put together a file.

Allison was glad, that she was able to assist the gentleman to choose the house he wanted to buy. He had been grateful.

It was the decision of the client, at the office, that represented them. Allison understood. She worked with real estate for some time. There was always the challenge, of trying to secure a loan. A client was always glad, when they received the best interest rate. Allison assisted many people.

Allison enjoyed the conversations that she has had over the past, several, years. There had been spouses, and partners, that talked of one another. There had been individuals that had been going through a divorce, and raised children in a different home.

Allison continued to think of all these things, as she waited for a gentleman that was supposed to meet her, at the office.

A half hour later, the gentleman came through the door. It had been the first time she had seen him. He had been pleasant.

The gentleman had begun to talk about his work as a college professor. He taught sciences.

Allison had begun to explain to him, the terms of his loan. He looked over the contract.

The gentleman asked Allison, several, questions about the contract, and she responded. Things continued to go well. The gentleman had agreed to the terms, and wanted to view the house, with Sue Anne. The gentleman invited, Allison to come along.

Allison agreed to attend the meeting with Sue Anne, and the gentleman. She did not have any additional meetings.

Allison made a call to Sue Anne. She agreed to meet them at the house.

When Allison, Sue Anne, and the gentleman arrived to the house, they walked along the outside. He turned his key, and they had gone inside.

When they had gone inside the house, there had been, several, furnishings.

The gentleman began to talk, about the things he planned to place, inside the home.

"Most of my furniture is new. I do have some things that I kept from my home".

Sue Anne had been talking, with, several, people, about the house.

Allison followed, as Sue Anne, and she were given, an official tour. The gentleman talked, in an attempt to give a glimpse of the way, the home would look. Allison admired the design.

By the time Sue Anne and Allison, finished looking at the house, and arrived inside the office, most of the day had nearly been gone.

Allison read another message from a client. Her office phone had begun to ring.

Allison had a feeling it was Jean.

"Allison, I' am calling to let you know, that I had to take Lynn to the emergency room. She somehow managed to twist her ankle, while she was outside. She will be fine. Lynn needs to stay off her feet for, several, days. She will continue to improve. You have to remember to schedule another appointment for Lynn, in several days. Her teacher had given me several assignments, for her to complete, for the rest of the week".

Jean waited for Allison to respond.

Allison knew that Lynn would have these situations, as she became older. Lynn enjoyed being acquaintances with her classmates. Allison was glad for that.

"Lynn, will need our attention for a while".

Allison promised Jean, that she had not planned to take any detours, on the way home.

"I do appreciate all you have done, for Lynn. I' am grateful, that you will watch her, until I arrive home".

Allison and Jean continued to talk. Allison had not noticed the time. Allison had been preoccupied on listening, to the information Jean was giving her.

"I did try to cheer Lynn up, by us playing board games. It worked. Her spirits lifted after that".

Jean waited, several, moments, before telling Allison, of her trip to visit her family.

"I think we will need to make, alternate arrangements for Lynn. She is not prepared to be home by herself. She has a recent twisted ankle. I do have a friend that maybe could assist you for the week. She primarily stays at home. Similar to me, Susan Mount Claire will have time to watch Lynn. You will need to ask Susan Mount Claire, at this time, if there is anything that will prevent her from taking the responsibility".

Allison thought that it would be a good idea for Susan Mount Claire to watch Lynn. She promised Jean that she would call the woman later that evening.

"Susan Mount Claire lives not far from the area I was born. We often talk with one another. Susan Mount Claire and I continue to remain acquaintances. Susan Mount Claire never raised any children. She volunteers with a group of children, several, times throughout the week. I do think that Susan Mount Claire would be great".

Moments later, Mark approached Allison. He asked her, if she had a difficult time completing any recent files. Allison told Mark, about her dilemma.

"Actually, I' am unsure if it is considered a dilemma. Jean gave me the contact information of the woman that will keep Lynn company for, several, hours after class".

Mark has told Allison in the past, that Gillian and he hired someone to watch David. We became familiar with them after a while.

"After, a while, the person developed, other obligations. Sometimes they are able to recommend someone different that could assist us".

Allison appreciated the support of Mark.

"Allison, my schedule at this time is busy".

Mark and Allison continued to talk for, several, moments. Things had been clearer for her. Allison does want to make sure that Lynn will be safe. When she was younger, she remembered her parents working. Allison's parents told her often, that they were glad they managed to spend time with her. She knew they worked hard. Allison would sometimes go into the city with Elise, and spend the day shopping. They sometimes, would walk around. Going into the city with Elise, was a reason Allison decided to begin real estate.

Allison noticed Mark starring at her. He had been waiting on her, to respond to a question.

"I mentioned that if you need someone to keep Lynn company, I could give you the contact phone number of someone".

Allison thanked Mark for the information. She waited a while inside the office. Allison heard that there may be an office meeting, that afternoon. She knew that she was supposed to meet with Lilia Bell. Allison looked at the time, before she ended her conversation with Mark. They both realized that there would not be a meeting.

Mary walked toward Mark, and asked him to answer a call from Gillian.

Mark answered the phone.

Mark began talking with Gillian.

Mark came over toward the desk of Allison.

"That was Gillian on the phone. Gillian wanted to let me know that she took David to the emergency room. He had an accident at school. David had been playing a sport with some of the children in his class. Someone accidently hit him in the nose. It sounds worse than it actually is".

Allison knew that Mark would go home after his last meeting. He planned to see his son. Allison knew that this would not be the last time that Mark would encounter an emergency situation with David, while he was inside the office.

Allison completed her meetings that day, before she went home. She had not wanted to be gone long. The three meetings had been brief. The second meeting had been the longest. Allison had to meet with a gentleman that was an investor. He had been communicating with a realtor at the agency. The gentleman specialized in commercial real estate. He had other investments that needed to be taken in consideration with his contract.

The gentleman applied for a loan for the house. Allison was to finalize the details of the loan with the gentleman.

Allison and the gentleman walked along a path inside a park located, several, blocks away from her office. He had been a gentleman in his seventies. The gentleman recently went through an operation within the past, several, months.

"The surgery I had is healing. I continue to be cautious at the things I do. I used to exercise often. Lately, wandering through a park has been the best form of exercise for me. Sometimes my daughter would come with me. There are, several, details, left to discuss, about the loan".

Allison and the gentleman discussed any possible issues with the house. She was not a realtor. Allison planned to follow the routine to finish the loan. The loan was the last process, before the clients could claim their property. Allison had meetings with investors in the past. They sometimes took more time, because of their, knowledge of real estate.

The gentleman told Allison more details about his daughter. That she at one time thought of becoming married, but changed her mind.

"She dated a gentleman for, several, years. They lived together, shortly after they began dating. They wanted that arrangement".

"My parents wanted the house to themselves. I had been living on my own for, several, months, when my wife and I began dating. I asked my wife to marry me one night, when we were out to dinner. We decided to ultimately become married at the courthouse. It saved us time. Later, we decided to move outside the city".

Allison listened to the story of the gentleman. He had done a lot of things in his life.

"Our daughter is the only child that my wife and I have. We are glad, that she decided to become a doctor. My wife and I, remain supportive of our daughter's career. Her career is important to her, and it keeps her busy. Our daughter told me that this was the reason she has not had any children. Allison, she is different, than I".

Allison had not mentioned Lynn. She somehow, had not thought it was appropriate. There were people walking around Allison, and the gentleman. They were in their own situations.

Allison had been dressed in business attire, because she had been at meetings, that day.

Allison looked through the wine menu earlier, because she thought that she might want to try a wine selection. She looked through the selections, and decided against them. Allison continued to drink from a glass of water. At this time, Allison knew that things would go well for the buying of the house, the gentleman, and his wife, had been interested in. She knew that they would need to continue their conversation some other time. It had become later, and she thought that she should return home, to see Lynn. Her daughter was to return to school, in the morning. She had been out for nearly a week. She told Allison the day before, that it will be nice to see her classmates again.

Allison arrived home.

Susan Mount Claire was home with Lynn.

"After dinner, Lynn fell asleep. I had not bothered to awake her, because I knew, that she needed to rest, for school tomorrow".

Allison and Lynn needed to awake early, and Susan Mount Claire had known that. She left their home.

Allison noticed that the house had been cleaned. She decided to go, and talk with Lynn.

"I fell asleep, moments ago. I hope that I do not become exhausted moving around with my cast. Moving back and forth is a little difficult".

Lynn completed the last of her assignment for class.

Allison felt bad that Lynn had to wear a cast. She hoped that her ankle would heal soon.

An hour later, Allison read a short story to Lynn. It reminded Allison and Lynn of when Lynn had been younger. Allison had not wanted to take up anymore of the time for Lynn to receive rest. Allison turned off the light, and watched Lynn, moments later, fall to sleep.

While Jean was visiting her family, Allison would take Lynn to school. Susan Mount Claire agreed, to be at their home, when Lynn arrived after school.

Zealand had been able to travel with Jean, because he had been an Australian Terrier. She had not wanted to part with him during the two week trip. After the trip, Zealand would be exhausted. It had been a while, since he, had been around Jean's family.

Allison had been glad, that she met Jean. She was a nice woman.

Allison had been downstairs waiting. Lynn came to let Allison know, that she had been ready for school. Allison had, several, meetings that day. She had a meeting with Lowell. Allison drove Lynn to school.

Allison waited for Lynn to walk inside the building with another student.

Allison drove to the office. She would meet with Mark, and they would walk inside the office together.

Mark finished parking into a parking space. He noticed Allison coming out of her car.

"When I see you in the mornings, you are organized. I spend time with my family in the mornings. Gillian is at home, because of the pregnancy. She is able to spend more time with our son, since she is not working".

Mark, and Allison, walked inside the office, and Allison missed, several, calls. She needed to return messages.

Darrell had not been inside the office. He had meetings, outside the office.

Allison planned to leave by early afternoon. She began to return messages. They were from prospective new clients, wanting to buy a house.

Mark was drinking a cup of coffee. He began to look through files. The coffee was working for him.

Allison waited for, several, minutes, after the last call, before she left the office. She needed to return later, to talk with a client.

Allison needed to meet with an executive of a company. He had been unsure, if he would buy a house from Delkes Realty. Allison was glad, that he was willing to think about using the realty firm. Allison had to meet with him, and give him the details of his contract. He had been thinking about buying another house for at least a year. The meetings with him had initially, been difficult. The gentleman traveled often. There had not been much information Allison had known of his career.

Allison looked at the clock, and realized that Mark had not come to visit her office. He must have been busy.

Allison left, after talking with the gentleman about the sale of his home.

Allison had not wanted to keep Lowell waiting, since he had not called her earlier that day. She assumed he was working.

Lowell had been prepared for the photo shoot, when Allison arrived, to the studio. He had his photography equipment arranged.

"Allison, I think we should create some photos with different types of clothes. These photos would be a good representation of my work, as a photographer".

Allison agreed.

She wore another piece of clothing from the wardrobe.

Lowell and Allison went through the photo shoot. The photos were coming out well. Lowell and Allison continued to work for at least another hour. She enjoyed the photo shoot. It was similar, to other photo shoots Allison had done.

Allison waited until the photo shoot was over, before she began to give her opinion.

Lowell told Allison, that he would finish developing the film, by the next morning. She would be able to visit him, in between any meetings that she may have. She would be able to look through the photos. Lowell told Allison, that he wanted to show them to, several, agencies.

Lowell had somewhere else that he had to be. Lowell told Allison that he would call her later that day. Maybe while she was inside the office.

Allison had two meetings. She was glad when she finished her day inside the office.

Allison waited a while inside the restaurant that she frequented. She drank a cup of coffee, before she went home. Her days ended at different times. This particular day, it ended late afternoon. Allison sat quietly reading the newspaper. She had no obligations at the time. Allison drove home.

Allison waited at home for Lynn and Susan Mount Claire to arrive home.

Lynn and Susan Mount Claire had come inside the home.

Lynn told Allison, that Susan Mount Claire and she had gone to visit animals at the park.

"After Lynn arrived home, she had been excited about spending time with the class pets. I thought that Lynn may want to visit some animals. I had a great time with Lynn. I know that Lynn will visit the animals with the class".

Lynn continued to talk to Allison about the visit Susan Mount Claire and she had with the animals.

Allison had been glad that Susan Mount Claire, and her daughter, enjoyed themselves.

Allison asked Lynn about her assignment.

Lynn told Allison that she left it inside the car.

Lynn retrieved her bag.

Allison told Susan Mount Claire about her day at the photo shoot.

"The photo shoot went well. It lasted longer than I thought. That is not necessarily a bad thing".

Allison told Susan Mount Claire, that the photo shoot lasted a while, because Lowell took additional photos. Next time they would be looking through the photos.

"I agree Allison that things will work out for you".

Susan Mount Claire handed Allison a souvenir that she and Lynn bought at the park.

Lynn had begun drawing.

Lynn told Allison that she finished her assignment that day. It had been, several, arithmetic equations.

Later, Allison, and Lynn began reading the newspaper. It had been similar events as the day before.

There had not been anything left that Allison or Lynn needed to complete that day.

Allison thought of her modeling career. She was glad that Lowell would continue to assist her.

Lowell had, several, meetings scheduled, that next day, from what Allison could remember.

Allison waited a while, before she called Lowell.

When Allison called Lowell, he had been working.

"Allison I had not expected to hear from you today".

They began a conversation. They talked of the first time he had seen her at the restaurant. Things had been difficult for him when he initially approached her. He had not wanted to give an impression, as if he, were following her. Lowell had been glad, that Allison had not accused him, of following her.

Allison and Lowell talked about his family. He told her they had not lived in the town. He had, several, acquaintances that did not live far from the town. He had been close to another photographer that lived in the city. He lived there for the past, several, years.

"I' am glad to be able to communicate with a photographer that is an acquaintance. Daniel lives a busy life now that he works for a lawyer. He enjoys his work. Daniel has been working with the lawyer for, several, years. He is considered an independent photographer. I' am glad that Daniel has become successful with his career decision. He has one employee working for him. Daniel and I, have a chance to talk from time to time. He usually talks with me about a difficult business situation. Daniel spends a lot of time on the phone".

Allison enjoyed being able to talk with Lowell. It took them away, from their difficult lifestyle. The evening was a nice time, to talk with him. They had many things, to talk about.

"The next, several, days, will be difficult for me. I have to meet with three colleagues. I have been working with them for a while. At the meeting, they will keep me updated on photography. At nine in the morning, is when I' am supposed to meet them. That is a good time for us".

"I have not seen other colleagues. At least we are all doing the things that we want to do. I have a great time as a photographer. As I mentioned before, I had not originally gone to school for photography. I majored in finance, thinking that I wanted to work in business".

"There were a lot of details to remember, when I first began photography. I became trained in photography. I continued to use, what I have learned".

Allison and Lowell continued to talk of photography. Allison learned a lot from him, thus far.

"Allison, if you want to try something different, then we could try different scenes, on your next photo shoot. The details are important".

Lowell asked Allison, about her decision, to not sell real estate.

Allison explained that her daughter had been born. Doing something related, freed up her time.

Allison was having a great time talking with Lowell, on the phone.

"I know that you want the best for Lynn. Before you realize it, Lynn will be in high school".

Allison hoped that Lynn would not grow up too fast. Allison accepted the idea, that Lynn was becoming older. Lowell and Allison had prepared to end their conversation, minutes later.

Allison was glad to talk with Lowell. She thanked him for the work, he had done for her. They worked well together.

When Allison and Lowell ended their call, she realized that her daughter had already gone to bed. Lynn was capable of going to bed on her own.

Allison thought the interesting part about modeling, was, that many people associated themselves, with the faces in publications.

Allison read through the news for, several, minutes, and then sat the newspaper down. Allison felt wariness, from her long day.

The next morning, Allison had taken Lynn to school. Within the three years that she lived in the area, she had become used to the familiar routine.

After Allison had taken Lynn to school, Allison ordered coffee at a restaurant.

Allison arrived home.

Edgar called Allison. He wanted to make sure that everyone was doing well. He had been adjusting to his new life. He had chosen to not become remarried. Edgar and Allison had been close to the same age. There was a three month difference in their ages.

Sara called Allison. Sara had not heard from Allison, and wanted to know about any upcoming plans that Allison had.

Sara told Allison the reason she called. She explained about an opportunity to display some of her gowns in a fashion event. The event would be held soon. It would allow people to see her new designs.

Allison told Sara at the time that she had not had any plans. She mentioned, that if anything came in the way of the event, that she would let her know. Allison did not mind driving into the city. After she agreed to be part of the event, Sara had given her the details.

Allison realized that it was time to pick Lynn up from school. They planned to bring Jean home from the train station. She had been scheduled to come home that day. The plans had not changed. Jean called Allison the day before at the office, to confirm the plans.

Lynn had been waiting for Allison outside the building. Allison assisted her into the car. Lynn continued to use crutches. Lynn talked excitedly about her day. She talked about the assignments she had been given. Lynn had been glad that she would be able to see Zealand.

Allison and Lynn arrived at the train station.

The train station was not crowded. There were, several, people walking around the terminals. Allison and Lynn noticed Zealand. Jean had him out of his carrier. Lynn had begun to ruffle Zealand. Allison held some of the luggage. Everyone walked to the car, and a valet attendant opened the back door to assist them in putting some of the luggage in the back seat.

Jean mentioned that she felt unbalanced from the train ride.

Lynn immediately began to ask her questions about her trip.

Jean answered her questions briefly. Jean told Lynn, that her family had been doing well.

"I was glad to see everyone since I had not seen them in over a year".

When Allison, Jean, and Lynn arrived to the home, Jean shared with Zealand, Allison assisted Jean to unpack.

Lynn was outside throwing a Frisbee with Zealand.

After a while, Jean and Allison began to prepare dinner.

After Jean and Allison finished cooking, they drank a cup of coffee.

Lynn had come back inside the home.

"Zealand will come inside, when he is ready".

Everyone had been enjoying their time. Allison drank more coffee. Everyone continued to talk about their day. Jean showed them photos of her family, and places they visited. It took them a while to go through some of the photos.

Zealand came, and jumped on the lap of Lynn. It made her laugh.

Jean went to answer her ringing phone. It had been a cousin making sure that she arrived home.

Jean talked, with her cousin for, several, moments, before ending the call.

Lynn had a long day, as she sat next to Zealand.

Allison suggested to Lynn, that they walk home.

Allison and Lynn left, so Jean could finish working on gown designs.

Allison called Lowell.

Allison told Lowell of the fashion event.

Lowell told Allison, that he would like to come to the event. He could possibly meet new contacts, and take, several, photos.

Allison could understand why Lowell would want to come to the event.

Lowell thanked Allison, for allowing him to come to the event. The fashion event had been good news for him that evening.

Lowell and Allison ended their conversation, several, moments later.

Lowell had a trip that was scheduled early that next morning. He planned to go into the city.

Allison arrived to the office an hour early. She wanted to read the messages that she received.

When Allison arrived to her desk, she found that there had been, several, messages. She waited to see if any clients would come to the office, before she left to an event. It would last for, several, hours. It was for real estate professionals. Some real estate managers decided they would attend. The speakers talked for almost half the day in the past. Everyone inside the office agreed to meet for an early brunch first.

Everyone in the office, at the brunch talked about recent files.

When Allison arrived to the event, she recognized, several, of the cars. Allison realized that other people had begun to arrive. Some of her colleagues had been at the table directly inside. Sue Anne and Mark had been there.

The group listened to some of the speakers, and the information had been informative. Every year that they had gone, things had changed a little in real estate. The audience began to participate. The audience had been given a list of current houses that were selling in the town. It would keep the offices busy for, several, weeks.

Allison finished a conversation with a banker, and she realized the event would end soon. She planned to go home afterwards. Allison had not known if she would return to the event the following year. The event had taken most of the day.

When Allison arrived home, things had been quiet. She realized that Jean and her daughter were not home. There had been a note from Lynn. The note was inside the kitchen. It explained that Ms. Anders and Lynn had gone to the far side of town to visit animals.

As Allison finished reading the note, Jean and Lynn were coming home. Jean drove her car into the drive.

Lynn walked toward Allison.

"We went to the park to visit the animals. I had not been able to see everything last week with Susan Mount Claire".

Lynn had been grateful.

"We had a chance to see a lot more today".

"When Lynn arrived home from school today, she mentioned her previous trip to me. The weather had been nice. I did not think it would be a bad idea to revisit the other side of town".

There had not been any souvenir for Allison.

Jean left.

Jean had gone to her home after she drank a glass of water.

Allison and Lynn were alone.

Lynn began an assignment. She remained quiet. Lynn asked Allison briefly, for assistance.

After Allison and Lynn had gone through the complete assignment, they were convinced that it had been completed correctly.

Allison took the day off, from her meetings. She drove Lynn to school.

Lowell and Allison went into the city where the fashion event was scheduled. They arrived early.

Sara found Lowell and Allison.

Sara immediately thanked Allison for coming.

Sara handed Allison a black gown that had chiffon material at the bottom. It was a well done design.

Allison thought the gown had been one of Sara's best designs. Allison mentioned this to Sara.

Sara had been distracted by the things going on.

Sara brought Allison to another room, and introduced her to, several, people that were also wearing formal wear.

"These are the other models".

Sara had given Allison a partner that was to walk on stage with her.

Lowell left Allison, and went into the crowd. He wanted to introduce himself.

Allison was sure that Lowell would have plenty of new contacts by the time they left. She could hear a lot of voices in the audience.

The group began to take their walk on stage. Allison had gone on stage with her partner. She wore the gowns that had been selected for her. She had been having a great time. The event was going fast. Allison felt less nervous, by the time that she went on stage a third time. Everything in the room, except the stage, had been dark.

Allison finished her last appearance. She left the stage. Allison felt she had done a great job.

Allison held a conversation with, several, of the models. They congratulated her on how well she had done. Allison mentioned that it had been somewhat new for her. The fashion event continued.

Allison had not known any of the models personally.

After the fashion event, Lynn found Allison.

"Allison you did a great job! I noticed everyone watching you".

Lowell had given Allison a kiss on the cheek.

"I think that Sara and you are popular women tonight. People have not let her leave yet".

Sara had been answering questions from the audience. She was comfortable with talking to the audience. Sara had not previously prepared her responses.

There were, several, business individuals that told Sara they would contact her at a later time.

Lowell talked again.

"I think that I should take, several, photos. I might be able to use them in the future".

Lowell left Allison, as she talked with, several, people.

The audience remained talking amongst themselves. The room remained occupied.

Jean and Lynn found Allison.

Allison had not known the amount of people that attended. She was glad, that Sara invited her, to be part, of the fashion event.

Allison told Sara that the fashion event was great.

Lynn had been standing next to Allison, when Lowell approached them.

Lowell wanted to introduce Allison to an advertising representative.

"He wants to take photos of you for a local advertisement. They are advertising a designer to be sold at, several, boutiques".

Allison was glad that she was able to spend her time modeling. It had become exciting for her.

"Allison I do see the best coming from you. It would be a pleasure, if you decided to be part of the advertisement. I will explain more to you sometime tomorrow, and that will give you a general idea about the advertisement. Maybe even in a phone conference. I wanted you to know about the opportunity".

"Allison, you are a popular person. I hope that you will want me to continue to assist you".

Lowell mentioned this to Allison.

The gentleman had introduced himself as Taylor, and requested a single photo to take with him. He reminded Allison that he would contact her at a later time. Taylor had given Allison a handshake, and left.

Lowell had begun to take photos of Allison, Jean, and Lynn. He finished after, several, minutes. Allison wore a blouse and skirt. They planned to have dinner at home, before Lynn would have to go to bed. The sun had begun to set as they left the event.

When Allison and Lynn arrived home, Jean came to their home to visit.

Lynn asked Allison questions about her modeling. She had not understood the career. Allison, Jean, and Lynn talked for about three hours. Jean had previously worked in boutiques for, several, years, before she retired. Jean continued to design for a while, when she moved into her current home.

When Allison began work, she remained focused on the files. She answered her phone.

Taylor had been on the other line. He wanted to go through an interview with her.

Taylor asked Allison, several, questions. After the twenty minute interview, he began to explain the advertisement, since she had never done any work for his agency. Taylor explained about the designer.

The agency planned to have Allison wear, several, different pieces in the wardrobe for the photo shoot. She would wear the best that fit her personality. Allison was expected to meet him at his studio that next day.

Allison had agreed.

Allison told Taylor, that he would have to change the time of the photo shoot around her schedule. She had been looking forward to the experience.

Allison finished eating her lunch at her desk that afternoon. She continued to think of their meeting scheduled the next day. The day went fast.

Before Allison left the office, she called Lowell, and told him of the plans.

Lowell told Allison to keep him posted on the details. He thought that it had been another great opportunity for her.

Allison knew that things would go fine. Allison had not felt intimidated by the situation. Taylor had been involved with advertising, for a while.

Allison mentioned her work inside the office. She told Lowell about, several, clients, that she had talked to that day.

"I communicate with the clients regularly, that way they could understand any issues they may have, when they are buying their house".

Allison had been the last person inside the office. It had been close to the fall holiday season, and most likely her colleagues had other obligations.

Allison and Lynn would celebrate with Jean. Allison had not had any meetings scheduled on that day. She would bring her daughter with her to the office. They would be able to go directly home, after they leave the office.

At this time, Allison thought, it would be nice to go shopping for the class party. Ms. Rosner wanted to have a party for the class the last day of classes, before the weekend.

Allison put away her folders, and walked cautiously to her car. There had not been anyone around that she was aware of. Allison thought of the incidents that had been occurring near the office. She safely drove her car away.

Lynn had been waiting on the doorstep for her.

"I walked over, several, minutes ago. I know that we were supposed to meet".

Lynn told Allison, that she enjoyed her day in class, and managed to finish a difficult assignment.

Allison drove, several, miles.

Allison knew, that driving for thirty minutes, Lynn and she would find many different places to shop. They were having a great time together.

Allison and Lynn arrived at the store.

The store had been busier than Allison would have thought. Lynn and she looked around. Lynn asked to try one of the cookies, and Allison reminded her that it would ruin her dinner. Afterward, Allison would not mind if Lynn decided to eat a cookie. They bought, several, things, before they left.

Lynn left Allison, when they arrived home.

Lynn wanted to spend time with Zealand. Lynn had not seen Zealand all day. She usually enjoyed playing a game of Frisbee with him.

When Lynn came inside, she mentioned that she had not begun her assignment for class. Lynn completed her assignment, and then decided to draw.

Allison and Lynn ate their dinner together. Lynn had been able to try one of the cookies.

Lowell demonstrated his creativity, as he took, several, photos of Allison. She had worn basic colors, and designs. She had been glad by the news that he had given her.

Another representative wanted Allison to be part of a different advertisement. The photo shoot would be advertising handbags.

"We would be glad to have you as part of an upcoming advertisement. I think it will be additional exposure for you. It would print for at least a month. After that, it could print again. Afterwards, you will have opportunities with additional photos that he needs to take".

Allison agreed to meet Lowell that day. He explained that it would last for an hour.

"I should be able to get the photos that I need with that amount of time".

Allison had gone through the rest of the day thinking about the details of the photo shoot.

Allison called to let Jean and Lynn know, that they should eat dinner without her.

Allison continued her work inside the office. Allison enjoyed modeling. She had been waiting for the opportunity to do something different. Allison knew, that she would not continue working in real estate.

Allison met with another realtor that day.

The realtor decided to buy a house from Mark. He told Allison, that his family and he spent a while deciding on the house. They discussed the type of interest rate that he was expecting. The rate, they finally chose, was similar to what he had in mind. The realtor and Allison spent about two hours discussing the contract, and the terms. After about an hour, they had finished their meeting.

Allison reminded Mark, that she would schedule the processing of the loan.

Allison had known within an hour that the documents, had been completed correctly, and accepted.

During their meeting, the gentleman talked of his schooling, and where he had completed his education. He had, several, other degrees, in other areas of business. The gentleman told Allison, that he did not have his own family. Instead, he had remained focused on his career in real estate. The gentleman offered to buy Allison something, in addition to her cup of coffee.

Allison declined.

The gentleman, continued to explain, the office he worked for. He worked there for, several, years, before he had been offered the management position. The gentleman decided to take the position. Afterward, with, several, sells he had become a partner. It had taken him several years, but he thought the company had been a good fit for him. His work continued to increase, as well as his salary. The gentleman told Allison, that some house sells, had not all gone smoothly.

Allison learned some things from the gentleman. He told her that he had known little about modeling. The gentleman sold, several, houses to designers. He had enjoyed meeting these people. He wanted, to say more, but he stopped.

The gentleman looked at his watch, several, times. He announced to Allison, that he had a prior engagement that he needed to go to. The gentleman promised Allison, that he would be in touch with Mark if he had additional questions.

"My mother had been visiting some acquaintances for the past three months. She has asked me to meet her at the train station, and assist her to put things away at her home. I' am unsure about the length of time she will be in the city. She has a meeting with a business associate. They have things that they need to discuss".

The gentleman and his mother had a close relationship. His career choice had assisted their close relationship. The gentleman told Allison, his mother was focused on her business. He enjoyed talking to Lynn about his mother. The gentleman told Allison, that his parents divorced when he was young. His mother has not left her career.

Allison thought in some ways the gentleman reminded her of Lowell.

When Lowell had been younger, he spent a lot of time with his father. His father would often come home early, that way he could spend time with Lowell.

The gentleman's father had worked as a photo journalist. He had not always talked of his career with his son. The gentleman mentioned that he had known about that part of photography, because of his father.

Lowell wanted to become a photographer, because he was interested in photographing people, and fashion. When he initially began his career it had been difficult. Not many people had known who he was. He spent years working with many people.

Lowell remembered the times that his father traveled with his career.

Allison called Lowell.

Allison wanted to tell Lowell, her thoughts about this particular client. Allison thought that even with the differences in their careers, that they had similar ways about their lives. Allison and Lowell had become close acquaintances.

"I think that my father may be completing some work. It has been at least a month, since I last talked with him. I feel bad, but I do know that he is busy. He works also as a consultant. The last we talked, my father had no intention of retiring. He is in his mid–sixties at this time. My mother is, several, years younger than he. They got along well for a lot of years".

"Anyway, I have to congratulate you. You work hard in real estate. You have done well in modeling".

Allison told Lowell that she had not heard from Taylor. She promised herself that she would call him soon. Allison told Lowell, that she would give Taylor a call, after they ended their conversation. She hoped they would be able to get the last of their details together.

"I agree Allison. You should give him a call. I have to do that often. Quite often, I have to sort through business arrangements. Sometimes I call, in order to finalize the details".

Lowell and Allison ended their phone conversation.

Allison called Taylor.

Taylor was busy, when Allison called him. He was completing a photo shoot.

"It is my fault Allison, that I have not called you. I work a lot of hours. I will call you at a later time today. As long as you are not busy. It may be, after you leave your office. I will be here at least another three hours. I hope that this is fine with you".

Allison told Taylor that it would be fine that he returned her call later.

Allison decided to visit Mark in his office. She had not talked with him in, several, days. Mark had been away from the office. He had meetings that whole week.

When Allison approached Mark, he had been on the phone with Gillian. She thought that she was going into labor. Gillian was due with the baby in two weeks. They were prepared for the birth. This had been what Mark told Allison. Things were going well thus far. Mark told Allison, that things had been busy for Gillian and himself.

"Expecting a child can be a busy time. You are never sure what to expect. You try to be prepared for the birth. The doctors tell you often that your child is fine. The truth is that you are unsure until after the child is born. Gillian has been resting for a while. That is the best thing for Gillian, at this time".

"Gillian plans to call the doctor, if her pains continue. I assume that they will go away. Gillian has been having bad morning sickness, for a while. That will continue to happen about every day, for the upcoming two weeks".

Allison knew, that the family would continue to do well.

Allison remembered Edgar, being concerned about Lynn, during her pregnancy.

A while later, Mark and Allison, began to talk about their lives growing up.

Mark mentioned that his parents, worked with real estate.

"Allison, my parents enjoyed their careers. That is why they began, to work in real estate".

Mark attended the university, for finance.

"Going to school for finance, is something that my parents chose to do. After they completed the university, they began real estate".

Mark knew a lot about real estate. His career had been difficult for him at first, when he began real estate. Gillian and he had been married early. Gillian had begun her salary inside an office, before Mark began working, inside a real estate office.

Mark had been concerned, for Gillian. Mark, and Gillian, had been married for many years.

Allison met Gillian, several, times, at different functions that the office, had given. Allison had known, that with a pregnancy, it could be hard to know, all the details. Lynn had been born, a week early.

Mark told Allison, that he would inform her, of when she would be able to visit Gillian and him at the hospital. Their parents' were going to be in town. Their parents' lived in other cities.

"Allison, my mother, had already made plans, to visit with us next week. She is going to stay home with Gillian, while I' am working. We waited a while, before telling our parents of the second pregnancy. We are raising David".

Allison heard her phone ring.

Allison answered the phone.

It had been Taylor.

Taylor apologized for not calling sooner.

"The agency that you recently worked with, wants to keep in contact with you. I hope, that I answered, all of your questions".

Allison told him, that he had.

"Allison, when I find work, that is good for you, then I will let you know".

Allison and Taylor ended their conversation.

Allison said goodbye to Mark, as she left the office.

Things ended well with the conversation Allison had with Taylor.

She understood the details of the advertisement. Allison drove home. She was ready to spend time with her daughter.

Allison arrived home.

Allison received a message from an agency that wanted her to contact their photographer. They wanted to complete a photo shoot with her. They had another magazine issue that was coming out, and wanted her to do some work for them. Allison wrote down the necessary information.

Allison walked next door. Her daughter had been outside with Zealand.

Allison talked with Jean. She told her that she had received the information. Jean had been glad for her.

"Allison, I' am unsure of what your future plans will be. I do know that Lynn is proud of you. She asks me all the time about your modeling. I tell her to ask you. I rarely have additional information to give her. You enjoy your career as a model, and things will go well".

They walked for, several, moments, before they drank a cup of coffee in the kitchen.

Allison appreciates the time that Jean and she spend together. She knew, that Jean had almost decided to become remarried years before. Things had been difficult after Jean broke away from her relationship. Jean told Allison, that after a while, she had become used to her different life. She continued to work for a while, at the job that she had in the city.

"After, several, years, I began getting used to the routine".

Zealand had been a nice dog for Jean to have. She had him for, several, years.

Allison and Lynn had arrived home.

The weather had become cold outside. The holidays were going to approach. The weather would change fast. Many magazines often put advertisements out for the holidays. They wanted to display new ideas, and designers.

Allison appreciated that Jean assisted her with Lynn. Allison thought of this often, as she spent time with Jean and Lynn.

Allison knew that at some time, Lynn would ask Allison to buy her a pet. Lynn most likely would ask for a dog.

Earlier, in the day, Lynn attended a concert with a classmate. It had been a chorus with the local high school. The school organized the concert for the past ten years. They had become popular. They recently changed some of their music.

Allison was glad that Lynn was becoming an acquaintance with her classmates.

Lynn told Allison of her time, that day at the concert. Lynn had never been to hear the concert before.

Things became quiet at the house, after Lynn began to draw. She stopped talking about the concert.

Around nine that evening, Lynn decided to go to bed.

Allison had been glad that Lynn was born. It is nice to see her have a great time with the people around her. Allison could remember being that way when she was younger.

Allison finished reading the newspaper.

Lowell decided to call Allison that evening.

Lowell told Allison, that it had been, the best time, to reach her. At this time, he knew that he would be able to talk with her. Lowell mentioned that there was an agency that would like to work with Allison. They would like to give her a contract for an advertisement that they are currently working on.

Allison agreed that it would be nice to meet with the agency.

"I thought that maybe we could spend some time obtaining updated photos of you. We need a small amount of time. Then afterward, we could develop, the film, together. The photos will be completed within a day or so".

Lowell promised Allison that he would give her a call. He would know what time the meeting will be. Lowell was thinking within the next two days.

Allison continued to listen to Lowell as he talked.

"I know that you enjoy your work".

Lowell paid attention to detail. That was a reason he wanted to become a photographer.

Lowell told Allison once, that sometimes it is easy to miss details. He planned to complete a lot more work in photography. Lowell intended to assist other people with their careers. He felt that some of the people he worked with expected him to be at every photo shoot opportunity they gave him.

Lowell mentioned that he had clients in the past that asked him, to take over another job of a photographer on a photo shoot.

The conversation ended with Allison promising to meet Lowell for the photo shoot, and have coffee, before she met with the individual about the advertisement.

"Allison, I do think taking the photos at this time will be a good idea. The agency will not want to view photos that are not recent".

Allison told Lowell, that she agreed.

Allison felt that Lowell often, had great advice. He was knowledgeable when he was assisting her, or when he was talking of a different person. Lowell continued to be a great source for Allison to understand modeling.

Mark had been on the other side of the office. He was looking at files on his desk.

"Allison, these are past loans that had not been completed. The loans usually have a reason for not being completed. Maybe some of the clients have gone other places. Allison, I' am sure you are already aware of some of these loans. I know that we try to keep the files updated".

"Gillian is due, at the hospital tomorrow. I' am not going to come, to the office. I made sure, that I was careful at not scheduling any appointments, for, several, weeks. I had not wanted to have, to cancel them".

Allison remained inside the office of Mark, to talk with him, about, several, other files.

Mark and Allison ended their meeting.

Allison went home to find her wardrobe for the photo shoot. She found everything that she needed. Allison noticed that Jean had already picked up the mail for her. She drove, to meet Lowell.

Lowell had been developing film, when Allison arrived.

"Allison, I have people asking me for assistance every day. Sometimes, they take the advice, that I give them".

Lowell found his camera.

Lowell and Allison talked, for, several, minutes, about the scene that would be best for the photos. Allison wore a sweater, with a dark skirt. It would look best, for the photo shoot.

Lowell took a series of photos.

Lowell asked the opinion of Allison.

Lowell took more photos.

Allison knew that the photography would come out well.

Lowell told Allison, that he would show her, how to develop the film, on her own. They talked about photography, as they worked together. Lowell and Allison had gone through the photo shoot, without any problems.

It had taken them, several, hours for the first part of developing. They created five different photos. Two of the photos, had been similar.

After Allison and Lowell finished working, Lowell told Allison, that he had, several, calls that he had to make, the next day.

"Allison, I do think, that you did a great job. At this time, we are almost finished developing the film".

Lowell handed Allison, a cup of coffee.

Allison promised Lowell, that she would join him for dinner, later that evening. Allison appreciated, that he had been kind to her.

"Allison, I understand that things will not always be easy. Sometimes, you have to complete things day by day".

Lowell reminded Allison that with his career, there had been plenty of things that he decided to do, differently than his parents. They were always supportive, of his career.

"I thought that I would do things similar as my father, because he enjoyed journalism. The truth is, that later, I began to learn how different, are careers were. He was considered a photo journalist. It kept him busy, in the news career. I think, that he tries to stay focused on journalism, because there are different things going on, quite often. I' am unsure of the last time, we talked of photography".

"Assisting people similar as you is rewarding for me. Besides, modeling is interesting".

Allison agreed. She enjoyed the creativity, with modeling.

Allison finished her coffee.

Lowell had not always, been a popular photographer. He worked at a restaurant. He had not completed college, at the time. After he became older, he worked with other photographers for, several, years. After that, people began hiring him, for work, as an independent photographer.

An hour later, Allison had arrived home.

Lowell called Allison.

Lowell wanted to remind Allison, that he would finish the work on developing the film. He talked, as he prepared a cup of coffee, at home.

Lowell always remembered details of his career, as a photographer.

"Allison, my lifestyle is busy at this time. That is why I' am glad, that I have an acquaintance like you".

Lowell mentioned this to remind Allison of their commonality.

Allison or Lowell had not been dating anyone.

Allison had been glad for Edgar, when he later decided to join a peace organization.

"When we talked of it, he told me that it had been something he wanted to do his whole life. He wanted to become part of the peace organization".

Edgar had been traveling with the peace organization for the past, several, years.

Allison asked Lowell to give her a moment to make sure Lynn was sleeping.

Allison opened the door, and her daughter had not awoken from her sleep. She walked toward the phone.

"Allison, I know that you will have a great interview tomorrow. The agency will assist you with more modeling opportunities. Give them your best interview. I will finish developing the film, this evening. Sometime tomorrow, before your interview you can pick them up. That way you will have something to show the agency. They will be talking with, several, other models. I' am unsure of the number of models that will be involved with the photo shoot. The agency does not select the people involved with the photo shoot at the beginning. Even if you are not involved in this particular advertisement, then you can work with them on another project".

Allison understood.

Several, years ago, Allison had not thought of modeling. She thought that it had not fit her personality. It was not until later, that Allison thought of designing, and modeling.

Allison decided to take the morning off, from the office. She remained alone, at home. Allison had taken, Lynn to school, that morning.

Allison received the photos, from Lowell.

When Allison arrived to the meeting, the secretary had been at the desk. The telephones had been ringing. The secretary answered, and began assisting the person with directions, to the office. She ended the conversation, and noticed Allison.

The secretary gave Allison a card, for her to write, her basic information.

Allison completed the card, with her information, within, several, minutes.

Allison was called to come through the doors for an interview. She held unto her photos. A gentleman had been sitting at his desk. He shook the hand of Allison. She handed the gentleman, her photos.

The gentleman glanced through the photos, and told her, that the photographer had done a great job.

As expected, the gentleman asked Allison, when she had taken the photos.

Allison told the gentleman, when she had taken the photos.

The gentleman listened to her answer.

"Even, if you are not in this particular advertisement, then I could let you assist me at a later time. The truth is, that I' am unsure, of what the scene will be, for the photo shoot. They are considering, several, options".

Allison listened.

The gentleman continued telling Allison about the agency.

The gentleman had been a photographer himself.

The gentleman enjoyed that Allison worked for Sara. He asked her about some of the designs.

Allison told the gentleman examples of the gown designs.

The gentleman and Allison began to talk about other topics. Things were going well for her.

Lowell told Allison, that if they ask questions for twenty minutes, then that was a good sign.

The gentleman never asked Allison the length of time that she had been modeling. She assumed that he had not wanted to know. They finished talking.

Allison left the meeting with the gentleman, shortly later.

Allison arrived to the office.

Allison needed to get some work done, before she planned to meet a prospective real estate client. The client had been patient with her, when she told them that she would need to reschedule their meeting.

Allison decided to drink a second cup of coffee.

Allison left the office.

Allison found the building. It had been a while, since she was in this particular part of town. It had been further from the office, than some of the other places she visited recently. The building was hidden. Allison knew that unless anyone had visited this part of town, that they would be unfamiliar with the building location.

Allison went inside the building.

Allison found a small office.

There had been a woman inside. She had been in the middle of a conversation, and ended it when she noticed Allison.

The woman greeted Allison.

The woman thanked Allison for coming to visit her. She introduced herself as Laurel, and told Allison that she owned her company for, several, years.

"We have had a lot of clients, since we have opened. Some of our clients have done advertisements for magazines. A model that I know had begun her career similar to you. That is why I invited you to be part of our upcoming advertisement. There is a boutique that is putting out a clothing line, and a new advertisement campaign. The advertisement will run for, several, months. I think it would be great for you, if you would want to work on this advertisement with us. I can see a lot of wonderful things happening for you. You have a lot of, dedication. That is a good quality. I' am unsure of the photographer that you have been using. He is able to continue representing you".

The woman asked Allison for her photos.

Allison had given the woman the same photos that she showed Alexander, at the other office. He had taken interest with the photos.

Alexander thought the photographer had done great work. He wanted Allison to take additional photos with another photographer that his company had been associated with. Alexander had been unsure, if they would need more of a selection of photos by a different photographer.

Laurel liked the work that Lowell had done as a photographer. Allison told her, that she wanted to sign the contract for the advertisement. She finished the meeting. It took Allison a while, to arrive to the office.

Allison arrived inside the office.

Mark had been at the office. He had been glad to see Allison.

Mark asked Allison about her business meeting.

Allison told Mark, that she felt that it had gone well.

Mark was glad for Allison.

"I' am unsure of why you had not chosen a different career sooner. Choosing a different career is something you obviously have wanted to do for a while. Everyone chooses their own path at what they do in life. At least you have decided to change your career now".

It was difficult to know where modeling would lead Allison.

Mark had been different than Allison. He wanted to continue to sell real estate.

Allison remembered how often Mark used to talk of the house that Gillian and he recently purchased. It was located, several, miles away from the office. Mark liked the design of the house.

"I lived in the city growing up. There had been long roads. The buildings were closer in proximity. I had not minded at the time. In college I decided to major in finance. I think that it was a good decision for me. As I mentioned before, that is what brought me into real estate. Even though I knew real estate, I needed to learn more about selling houses".

Mark spent more time in real estate than many people Allison knew.

Allison and Mark talked of the local events for, several, moments, before she went back to her desk to make several phone calls.

Allison had a message from Hansen.

Allison had been selected to do the recent advertisement. Hansen knew of another current advertisement that was going on. He thought that it would be great for her.

Allison was to call him within an hour, if she had been able to. Allison decided that she should call Hansen.

As Allison planned to call Hansen, her phone had rung.

It had been Laurel contacting Allison, after their meeting.

"The company is glad, that you choose to complete, the advertisement".

Laurel apologized for being brief. She told Allison, that she had, several, calls, to make. Laurel asked Allison, to meet her inside her office, that next afternoon.

"The photographer will take some photos of you. It should not take, too long".

Allison thanked Laurel.

Laurel ended the conversation with Allison.

Allison called, the desk of Mark.

Mark was glad, that Allison would, be able to complete an advertisement. He suggested that they have a cup, of coffee. Mark would bring it to the office, and they could, finish their work.

Allison thought, that it sounded, to be a good idea.

Allison filed away some work, and Mark returned to the office, within, several, minutes.

Mark had two cups of coffee with him. He congratulated Allison, as they drank their coffee, and completed their work.

Allison thanked Mark, as she left, the office, for the day.

When Allison arrived home, she went directly, to the home of Jean. The sun had been out. Jean had been outside, organizing her garden.

Allison could hear, Jean call her, as she walked toward her.

When Allison was close enough to Jean, Allison, told her about the interview.

"I' am glad, that you were able to obtain, this advertisement".

"The advertisement, will display for, several, months. After the photo shoot, they may have me continue, to work with them".

Jean congratulated Allison. Things had gone well, thus far.

Allison planned to call Lowell, and inform him of their decision. She would be able to complete the advertisement.

Allison assisted Jean, with, several, simple tasks.

Lynn kept herself busy, throwing Frisbee, with Zealand. He appreciated the attention. Allison thought that it would be nice, to take Lynn to buy her own dog. She told Jean, that she had planned to do this, when Allison, talked with Jean, on the phone earlier.

Allison talked with Jean for an hour.

Allison found Lynn, and told her that they were going to visit the animal shelter. She wanted her to find a dog at the animal shelter. When they walked toward the car, Lynn continued to wave to Zealand. They arrived to the car, and Allison drove over an hour into the city.

When they arrived to the animal shelter, Allison and Lynn walked inside.

A young woman greeted them. She offered to show them around. The woman showed them, several, animals including cats.

Afterward, since Allison and Lynn wanted to buy a dog, the young woman showed them the dogs that were available.

Lynn noticed an Australian Terrier that looked similar to Zealand. She began barking at them playfully.

"Allison, I think it would be nice to have a dog similar to Zealand".

The young woman brought the dog to them.

The young woman handed the dog to Lynn.

Lynn decided that she wanted the dog. The Australian Terrier was similar in age, as Zealand.

The young woman told Allison and Lynn, that they were able to buy the dog.

When Allison and Lynn, left the animal shelter on Tenth Avenue, Lynn had been glad. The Australian Terrier had been inside of her carrier.

Lynn told Allison, that she wanted to name her Sammy.

"I enjoy this name. Do you think that she will learn her name"?

Allison agreed with the name of the dog.

Allison assured Lynn, that Sammy would learn her name.

The animal shelter had not had a lot of information on the parents. The young woman told them, that since the owners had not provided any additional information, it made it difficult to know details on the dog. They knew she had been an Australian Terrier.

Allison would assist Lynn to take care of Sammy. Lynn knew at times, Sammy would wander with Zealand.

Allison and Lynn arrived home.

Lynn took Sammy out of her carrier.

Sammy began to wander, and had a great time. She had been healthy, and had continued to remain playful.

Later, Sammy took a nap.

Allison and Lynn had gone to the local store.

At the store, Allison and Lynn bought dog supplies for Sammy. They bought her food, and, several, blankets. The blankets were great for Sammy. Allison and Lynn bought a new camera.

Allison began to take, several, photos of Sammy. She had been sleeping at the time.

Allison and Lynn had begun to prepare dinner. They decided to make stew. Allison and Lynn made stew occasionally.

Similar to Zealand, when Sammy noticed Allison and Lynn eating, she began to walk toward the table.

Sammy jumped on Lynn's lap.

Sammy had been aiming to go toward the plate of food. Lynn had been concerned about the dog eating her food. Lynn found the dog food that Allison and she brought home.

Sammy agreed to eat the food that she had been given.

"At least we know that Sammy does like the food that she is eating. I have heard of some house dogs that do not like to eat the food that is meant for them".

Lynn mentioned that she wanted to bring Sammy over to Zealand, and they could play together.

Allison previously asked Jean if Sammy could play with Zealand.

Jean had been outside the next day waiting for Lynn to arrive outside the school building. She waited outside most days, as long as the weather had not been bad. It was nearly approaching the middle of the fall. In the town, the snow had not fallen.

Jean and Lynn arrived home.

Sammy needed to be walked.

Sammy had been sleeping. She would become used to the routine.

When Sammy awoke, Jean and Lynn walked her. The whole time Jean gave Lynn pointers on how to raise and care for her dog. Within an hour, they completed their outdoor walk.

When Jean, and Lynn arrived home, Sammy, and Zealand became active. They began wandering around outside. Sammy and Zealand enjoyed the cool air.

When Allison arrived home, Sammy had been inside. Lynn had been talking with Jean. She was even happier these days, since they had Sammy. Jean joined them for dinner.

Allison told Jean and Lynn that she had a long day. She described a car accident that occurred near the real estate office building. Everyone involved had been fine. Allison referred to the details that she had been given. Her colleagues and she were able to piece some of the details together, based on what they learned from the police.

An older woman had been taken to the hospital. The emergency personnel wanted to make sure, that she would be fine. The woman had not been injured, only, that her body might be in shock.

A driver attempted to leave the scene of the accident. The police had been looking for him. They were unsure of where he could have gone. The police were hoping that someone would recognize him, and they could locate the gentleman.

Other than hearing about the car accident, Allison's day had been her normal routine. She had to meet with a realtor that day. The meeting lasted for a short time.

Allison spent most of her time inside her office. Several, realtors were inside the office. Most of them have spent at least three years together. Real estate had not been new for them. They arrived primarily from other offices.

Allison, Jean, and Lynn finished their dinner. Jean said goodbye to everyone. She wanted to complete some work at home. Jean wanted to begin designing gowns again. She told Allison that she remembered some of the details, from when she had designed in the past.

"I completed design work in the past. I completed numerous of sketches. Maybe if you have time, then you could assist me with, several, of the designs. The designs will be simple at first".

Allison would assist Jean with her designs. She walked her to the door. Allison had been glad. They were both working on similar goals. This will be something that will be good. Allison was interested, that Jean decided to complete more gown designs. She had shown Allison some of her previous gown designs.

Allison thought of the details of the car accident near the real estate building. The outcome was not apparent in the local newspaper. Allison hoped that the woman would continue to be fine. Allison sometimes came in and out of the building, several, times throughout the day.

Allison noticed Sammy sleeping. She stayed inside during the day. Jean and Lynn took Sammy for a walk, when Lynn arrived home from school. Sammy was adjusting to her new home, and liked everyone around her.

Allison had planned to stay home that following day. She wanted to make, several, appointments for Sammy. Allison wanted Sammy to see the veterinarian, and a pet groomer. Allison would mention this to Lynn on her way to take her to school.

Lynn awoke earlier than usual. She found Allison reading the newspaper. Lynn mentioned that she had been ready for school. They decided to drink a cup of tea, before they left their home.

After Allison took Lynn to school, she made two calls, and two appointments. The offices were eager to be able to see Sammy.

Doctor Edward Johnson asked Allison, several, questions about Sammy. He told Allison, that Sammy had been healthy. Doctor Edward Johnson told Allison, that Sammy had been lucky to find a safe home.

Later, Allison took Sammy to a groomer. Joyce Eagleston had not been far from the previous appointment. Sammy had been patient with Joyce Eagleston.

With a lot of people caring for animals, the veterinarian and groomer, had not been difficult to find.

Allison noticed the, several, paintings that were framed on the wall of the groomer. They were of impressionist art. It was one of her favorite forms of art. Allison waited for Sammy to finish her appointment. Afterward, Joyce Eagleston handed her to Allison, in her carrier. Sammy was content when Allison and she left the office of the groomer.

Lynn was glad to see Sammy, when Allison and Sammy arrived to the school. She had been in the backseat. Lynn told Allison about the plans that she made with an acquaintance from the class. They planned to see a high school chorus perform. Allison promised Lynn, that she would contact her parents. Lynn was glad with that response.

"It would be nice if we could bring our pets to school. Maybe Lowell will take a photo of Sammy for me, and I would be able to bring it to class. I' am sure my classmates would like to see a photo of Sammy".

Lynn began to play Frisbee with Sammy.

Jean was spending time with, several, acquaintances' that day, since she had not had to stay with Lynn. She found the extra time rare. Jean had been glad that she was able to devote her time to designing gowns over the past, several, weeks.

Lynn held Sammy.

Lynn told Allison, that Sammy should spend time with Zealand tomorrow.

Allison agreed with her.

Allison went to the photo shoot, that next afternoon. She waited for someone else to finish their photo shoot. The photographer had to take, several, photos.

Moments later, he mentioned to Allison that his name was Randall. He had been working on the advertisement for, several, weeks. The company is trying to put the details together.

Randall had been patient with Allison, while they continued the photo shoot. He explained the way things were supposed to look. Randall mentioned that sometimes the photo shoot took longer, depending on the advertisement.

"Allison, the company has been going back and forth with details the whole time. Sometimes they ask me for ideas. That is rare. For the most part, I have to go along with what the company decides. I do not blame them for being indecisive, because it is their advertisement. Next, they will decide on how long the advertisement will run. I have visited different places within the past, several, years. I have met, and became familiar with, several, designers".

Allison told Randall, that she recently met, several, designers.

"I understand Allison. I think, in time, things will become easier. I think a lot of people wait for an opportunity to expand their career. I think you will continue to enjoy modeling, since you are patient".

Allison could understand the viewpoint of Randall.

He asked her about her personal life.

Allison responded, with telling Randall about her daughter. He had not known that she had a daughter or anything else about her personal life. Allison told Randall about Lynn's adjustment to her new class.

Things became easier, when she realized that there had been a classroom pet. Allison mentioned that things were going great for her daughter. Allison told him, that Lynn enjoyed drawing.

"At this time, your concern is probably Lynn doing well in school".

Allison was glad that Lynn enjoyed school.

Allison spent the next hour taking more photos. When they completed, Randall thanked her for her time, and hard work.

"The details of the photo shoot will be settled shortly. The advertisement will be completed in two weeks. I do not think that this will be a big advertisement. In, several, years, things will be moving even faster with your modeling career".

Allison knew that she would continue to gain experience with modeling.

They finished their work, and Randall reminded Allison, that he appreciated her patience.

Allison drove to the office.

When Allison arrived inside the office, the agency called, to ask her to be a part of another advertisement.

Allison agreed.

The agency liked Allison.

Allison told Mark about her work.

Mark asked Allison more questions about her work as a model.

Allison reminded Mark, that she was concerned about being too busy. She wanted to be able to spend time with Lynn.

Mark had not known of any other incidents around the building. He remained gone from the office, when Gillian had given birth. Mark spoke of Gillian, and her mother Madden. She agreed to remain in town for a while, to assist Gillian and Mark. That would give them enough time to get used to work again.

"Gillian is anxious to get back to work. She has been waiting for some time, to have part of her daily routine normal".

An hour later, inside the office, Mark and Allison were discussing, several, client files. They planned to work with them, to sell their houses. Shortly afterward, Mark had a meeting, and had to leave the office.

Allison had been alone inside the office. She wanted to make sure that the building had been secure. Allison had gone around the building, and checked that the doors were locked. She was supposed to meet with another client in the morning. Allison knew that it would be a brief meeting. The woman that Allison was meeting with had been expecting to be in her new house, within, several, days. Allison planned to make several calls, so the loans would be processed.

Jean and Lynn had been waiting for Allison, to arrive home. Allison had enjoyed the inside, of the home. Jean had spent time, redoing the kitchen. The living room consisted of beige, and cream. Jean had areas, where she placed, finished wooden furniture.

Sammy and Zealand, had been sitting quietly, next to each other. They watched everyone around them, in conversation.

"Allison, I hope that you do not mind, that Sammy ate. I fed Sammy and Zealand, their dinner. I had not wanted them, to disturb our dinner".

The conversation focused on Lynn, and the day she had at school.

"Ms. Rosner volunteered the class to complete some projects for the town".

Allison had been glad for her daughter. Ms. Rosner enjoyed her profession. Allison wanted to let Lynn finish talking, and had not disturbed her. She thought about her own, previous education. Allison enjoyed spending time, with her daughter. Edgar was involved in a new career, and Lynn seemed, to understand that.

Since Edgar and Allison divorced, Allison had not been spending as much time at work, as in the past. She has been able to spend more time, with Lynn.

Allison knew, that Lynn had been enjoying the time they had been spending, with Jean. Lynn was young. Allison knew that recently, with modeling, things had changed slightly. She joined, into the conversation.

Lynn talked of the young boy, Jacob. He continued, to get into trouble.

"I enjoy everyone in my class, but I have to say, that I like being at home".

Allison explained to Lynn, that she would eventually, complete more activities with her acquaintances in class.

Sammy had begun to walk toward Lynn slowly. She began barking, until Lynn picked her up.

"Sammy, will continue to cheer you up. She is doing a great job thus far. According to the veterinarian, she has a birthday soon. We can choose a day to celebrate".

Lynn agreed with the plan to celebrate the birthday of Sammy. She brushed Sammy's hair, before she sat her down. Lynn thought originally, that it would be difficult to take care of Sammy.

Once Lynn began drawing, Allison decided to make a call to Lowell. She had not talked to him in, several, days.

When Allison called Lowell, he told her that he had arrived home, several, minutes before.

"Things were hectic for me today. I had gone into the city to complete some work. Several, of the photo shoots, I' am working on, are around this area, throughout the month".

Lowell continued, with a comment about his personal life.

"I think that my personal life is where it should be, at this time".

"That is a great way, to look at your life".

"Lately, I have become focused on my photography business".

Lowell asked Allison, if she heard from Hansen or anyone at the agency, since the last photo shoot.

Allison reminded Lowell, about the conversation she had with Hansen.

Lowell promised Allison, that Hansen would be contacting her, about additional work.

"They will be contacting, you soon. They have plenty of work, for you. They will want to continue to have meetings, with you. They want to make sure everything, goes well".

Lowell continued talking, about his work.

"Allison, the people that I work with, continuously, give me, a new perspective, on a photo shoot".

"I learn things from, you Allison. We spend a lot of time communicating. I know, that you intend to model, for a while".

Allison appreciated the compliment, from Lowell.

"I know that you do a great job, as a photographer, Lowell".

"I think that we ultimately have great careers. I think, that you should continue to perfect, your portfolio. I know that once you continue to work with the agency, they will continue to assist you with your career".

"I have added your photos in my portfolio. Maybe someone will want to talk with you, in reference to me".

"It took a while, but the photos came, out well".

Lowell mentioned to Allison, that he would talk with her within, the next week. He said this to her, before he ended, their conversation.

"Allison, someone tampered with files in one of the other offices. Someone broke inside the law office, several, doors down. There were files stolen belonging to clients. The police responded quickly. Especially, because of the incidents that has been recently occurring in the area. They will soon question people that the lawyer associates with".

Sue Anne was concerned, as she told this to Allison.

"I' am glad that we have not had any incidents occur in this office. I do not think the office needs to be concerned. We have, several, files that we will work on today. Afterward, we will lock the files away".

Sue Anne began looking at a file.

Allison remembered that she had to call a client to schedule a meeting. She continued to look through the file that contained his information. Allison noticed that the client had been a doctor. She remembered the doctor was relocating his practice. Allison had planned to call the client in a short while. She wanted to complete, several, tasks first. Allison worked, until Mark approached her.

"I came in late. Sue Anne told me what happened inside the other office. Gillian was experiencing some pain. She thought that it may be due to the recent birth. If anything worse happens, I will let you know. I plan to leave the office at ten thirty for a meeting".

Mark left her office, after he explained the recent events within his family to Allison. She had some work to complete, but knew the situation with Gillian would improve.

Allison wanted to spend time arranging her modeling portfolio.

Lowell had given Allison some suggestions. She had ideas, of what she wanted to add.

Allison arrived at the restaurant.

Allison ordered coffee, as she put together her materials. She enjoyed her photo shoots, but did not enjoy the uncertainty, of the work. It initially had been confusing, but Allison had become used to modeling. It was an opportunity to do something different. She looked, at, several, photos.

When Allison returned to the office, there had been a message, from Mark. He wanted to let her know why he left, the office, in case he received any phone calls, from clients. Mark told Allison, that he had received a call, from Gillian. She decided to visit, the doctor. Gillian had been experiencing pain that had not, gone away. Gillian had been taken to the hospital, by her mother Madden, and Anne. Mark told Gillian, that he would meet them, at the hospital.

Allison called Jean.

Allison told Jean, of the events with Mark, and his family. She planned to go to the hospital, and see the, new baby.

Mark and Gillian talked with Allison. She told them, she had not had to see any clients the remainder of the day. She wanted to visit them at the hospital, because Mark and Gillian had been supportive of Lynn and her. They explained that David had been at home with a neighbor.

Gillian talked.

"David might have become, impatient being, at a hospital. We will not be at the hospital long. Everything is better, with me. David needs someone to watch him, every day. Once my parents come back into town, it will give them the opportunity to spend time with David, and Anne".

Mark and Gillian continued, to talk with, the doctor.

Allison explained that she needed to leave. She wanted to be home, before Lynn went to bed.

Allison found the cafeteria. She wanted to eat, her dinner.

There had been the hospital personnel, walking through the cafeteria.

While Allison sat inside the cafeteria, she noticed the newspaper. She found the fashion section, and noticed the photos. There had been many designs. Allison noticed many models in dresses, and suits. The photo shoots had been, well done. Most of the designs of the fashion consisted, of seasonal patterns. It had been, several, days, since Allison had been able to look through the fashion. She thought, about her own career.

Allison wondered if the family of Mark, and Mark remained, at the hospital.

When Allison arrived home, Jean had design material sprawled around her living room.

"I wanted your opinion, on the gown, that I' am working on".

Allison looked at the gown, and thought the detail, had been great.

Allison told Jean, that she thought the design was coming, together nicely.

"If you had more time, then I would have asked you to assist me. I will bring this gown to, several, boutiques, in the area. Maybe they will ask me, to make more designs, for them".

Jean felt that things have been going well so far, with this particular gown.

Allison apologized, for arriving home late.

Jean understood that Allison wanted to visit, Gillian, and Mark.

Allison reminded Jean, that she enjoyed the design. She told her, that she would be willing to assist her with her business, when she could.

Jean thanked Allison.

"I' am always working on, new designs".

Allison and Lynn walked through the door, at their home.

Allison made warmed tea.

Lynn told Allison, about her day, at school. She had been unable, to understand why Jacob behaved the way, he had. Lynn told Allison, that one day, he will behave correctly.

Allison and Lynn enjoyed their time together. At about ten that evening, Lynn was sleeping, and Allison decided to finish reading the newspaper. There had been headlines that had, been running.

That next morning, Allison had gone to the office.

Sue Anne was at the office.

Mark called Allison, and said that everything had been going well with Gillian.

"The doctor told Gillian, that she needs to rest".

The doctor told Mark and Gillian, that Anne was growing, and was healthy. She had gained another two pounds.

Allison promised Mark, that she would let everyone in the office know, that everything was well. She was sure that they would be glad for him.

Mark reminded Allison, that he had not known when he would return to the office. He told Allison, that his parents planned to stay for a while to assist with Anne.

Allison visited Hansen at his office.

Hansen had, several, envelopes on his desk. They consisted of photos that Allison had given to him.

Hansen reminded Allison that the advertisement that she recently completed, would display for a while. He began to explain an advertisement that he thought would be good for her.

Allison thought that the advertisement would be great for her.

Hansen told Allison that she should meet him at his office that next day. She would be able to get the information of her photographer, so she could schedule an appointment with him to complete the photo shoot. It would take them, several, hours to complete the photo shoot.

"It is nice that you are with our agency. I wanted to thank you, ahead of time for doing the photo shoot".

Allison left the office, of Hansen. She had not had any work to complete at her office, and decided to go home.

Jean and Lynn had been waiting, for Allison. Jean had design materials sprawled around, the home.

"I was in the middle of working on another design. I' am unsure if you would be able to wear one of the gowns I designed, at your upcoming photo shoot. It would assist me to show people my new designs. I have not decided on the cost of the latest gown".

Allison had been glad for Jean. She told her about her meeting, that next day with, the photographer.

Jean congratulated Allison, on the upcoming photo shoot.

Allison would ask, if she could wear Jean's design, in her photo shoot.

"The agency has promised that they would choose work that would allow me to use more of my, own ideas".

"This particular advertisement will run for, a while. It is difficult to say the actual time. I will continue working with the agency. I would not want to stop the contract at this time. It will not be good. At nine tomorrow, is when I' am supposed to meet the photographer. Everything will go well. The name of the photographer is Floyd. He has been working with photography for over fifteen years. His work has turned out well. He has completed a lot of work in photography".

Allison asked Jean, how she created the particular design.

"I used three different patterns and two different fabrics".

Jean could tell that Allison had enjoyed the particular gown. It was obvious, that it would turn out well.

"At this time, it is almost completed".

Lately, Jean had been able to spend most of the day working, until Lynn arrived home, from school. After Lynn arrived home, is when she took a break from her work. Lynn often talked about, the latest details in the class.

That particular day, Lynn mentioned, that the class hamster died. Some of the children had been heartbroken. Lynn then told the class about Sammy, and the class had become excited. Lynn told Jean, that most of the class has a, pet at home. Ms. Rosner suggested that the class should get another hamster. Lynn was content with, this idea.

Lynn walked toward Jean, and Allison. She had been followed by Sammy, and Zealand. Lynn, Sammy, and Zealand had been playing

Frisbee. Lynn had come to talk with Jean and Allison. They welcomed her into the conversation.

Jean reminded Lynn of the conversation earlier about the new pet.

"Ms. Rosner arranged for the class to bring pictures of their pets".

"I' am glad for you Lynn", Jean told her.

Ms. Rosner arranged for the class to bring photos of their pets.

Lynn noticed the gown. She decided to comment on the gown.

"The gown will be beautiful".

Jean thanked Lynn for the complement on the gown.

Lynn thought the gown had been a nice design. She enjoyed the material.

The next day, Allison met with the photographer Floyd.

Floyd had been waiting for Allison. He approached her, and explained that he wanted to discuss the layout of the photo shoot.

Allison showed Floyd the gown that Jean designed.

Floyd agreed to take, several, photos of Allison in it. He was unable to promise her that it would be part of the advertisement.

"The agency chose a designer that they will use".

Allison told Floyd, that she understood if the gown that Jean designed was unable to be part of the advertisement.

Floyd told Allison, that the driver would drive them around to, several, places for the photo shoot. They would visit an outdoor garden that day. The locations were located outside the city. They would not have to go far.

Allison followed Floyd to the car.

The driver and the car had been waiting near the front entrance.

Floyd and Allison arrived to a small park.

"We have arrived where I want us to be. I need, several, minutes to set up the equipment. After we finish here, then we will go to the next location".

The driver left with the car, and planned to return later.

"The agency sometimes chooses to use a driver during photo shoots. When there is a driver, I usually receive little details of the location of the photo shoot".

Floyd continued to set up his equipment. Allison had worn a wardrobe piece for the photo shoot.

"Allison, I hope that you are prepared to wear, and put on your own makeup. I assumed that I had not needed anyone to assist you with your makeup. Your makeup will not be noticeable in the photo. If that were to happen, it may become distracting".

Floyd and Allison concentrated on the photo shoot. He began with the first set, of photos.

Allison wore the gown that Jean made.

Floyd told Allison, that he liked the design, of the gown.

"I do hope that they use one of the photos from this particular set of photos. The gown is, well done".

"I will recommend that one of the photos with the gown, be used in the advertisement. I cannot guarantee that it will happen. We can try our best to finish the photo shoot today. We should leave soon. We have additional places to go. We need to take more photos".

Allison understood that Floyd, and she needed to leave the park. The photo shoot would be completed soon.

Floyd began to take more photos, for a half hour. Floyd assured Allison that he would give her a copy of the photos, once he developed the film.

Allison thanked Floyd for being patient with her, during the photo shoot.

Floyd and Allison talked for a while, after they finished their work. He told her of several, other projects that he was working on. Allison had enjoyed hearing about his work. It would take another week to complete.

"I had a project that lasted nearly a month about half a year ago. Those photo shoots generally were in a different town. I' am unable to leave those jobs once, they begin. I have to take photos of different scenes. It depends on the photo shoot of what the work will, consist of. I' am accustomed to working in different places. When I have to travel, someone will call me, and I may be expected to take a train the next day".

It had been approaching late afternoon. Floyd and Allison took two more photos. Allison had worn another wardrobe piece.

Floyd had begun packing his equipment. He wanted to be able to complete the photo shoot. Floyd knew that the rest of their photo shoot, that day would take less time.

Allison felt that the photo shoot, that, Floyd, and she had been working on, was one of the longest photo shoots, she had completed. It lasted longer than she thought.

Floyd and Allison had arrived to their last destination. On the last set of photos, he gave her the option of taking more photos with the gown she brought with her.

Allison decided to take more photos with the gown Jean designed.

"Models like to use the copies of the photos I give them, in their portfolio".

Floyd and Allison walked toward the car, and the driver had been waiting for them. The driver took them back to the studio.

Allison drove home, once Floyd and she arrived to the studio.

Floyd traveled behind her, so he could meet Allison's daughter.

When Lynn noticed Allison, she walked toward the car. She noticed Floyd. She starred at him, as she stood next to Allison.

Floyd acknowledged Lynn.

Lynn gave Floyd her hand to shake.

Floyd and Lynn shook hands, as Floyd told Lynn his name. Lynn wanted to learn more about him.

Floyd told Lynn that he was a photographer for Allison. They finished taking, several, photos.

Floyd could tell by the expression that Lynn had on her face, that she thought he wanted to date Allison.

Floyd asked Lynn, if she had any close acquaintances in the class.

Lynn informed Floyd about the young boy in the class that enjoyed attention from the class.

The conversation focused on Lynn.

Floyd had not minded talking about Lynn. He related with her. Floyd mentioned to Lynn about his studio in the city.

Lynn began to let her guard down.

Jean had been watching Sammy and Zealand.

One of the questions he answered for Lynn, Allison had been wondering.

Lynn asked Floyd, where he lived.

Floyd told Lynn that he lived in the city, not far from his office.

Floyd reminded Lynn that he needed to go home, and that he would talk with Allison, and her at a later time.

Allison explained in more detail to Lynn, that Floyd and she were acquaintances. He had been an assistant with the agency. Allison mentioned to Lynn, that she had taken more photos that day.

Allison had not said much to Jean.

Allison and Lynn walked toward Jean. She had given Zealand and Sammy their dinner.

Jean and Allison remained talking about her gown designs. Jean wanted to complete, several, before she sold more to a boutique. She wanted Allison, to keep the gown that was used in the photo shoot. Jean had been glad that Allison had worn it in her photo shoot. Things had been going well for her. Jean had been glad for Allison, and herself.

"I' am glad that you are here to assist me with my work. I know that your schedule has increased, since you began modeling".

Jean had been talking to Allison.

"I created, several, patterns. When I first began sewing, it took me a while, to complete something".

Jean had been glad, that Allison understood designing gowns.

"I have to say, that I was primarily focused on clothing in the past. The, several, items that I made disappeared, over the years. I personally rather focus on designing gowns, at this time".

Jean hoped that her gowns would become popular.

"I talked with Marian earlier. She owns Marian's Boutique. She gave me additional assistance. Marian said that she would talk with, several, different people. She would see if they would sell another gown, or if there were any shows that would be able to sponsor my gowns. Marian agreed that she would contact me, if she receives any information".

Jean reminded Allison that if she had known anyone interested, if she would remind them, that she is a gown designer.

Jean and Allison began to sew material on the sides of the particular gown that Jean was completing.

An hour later, Jean, and Allison continued working, while Lynn continued to draw. She had been drawing a woman, in a dress.

Allison noticed it, and complemented her daughter. Allison thought it had been good experience, for her to use different, artistic techniques.

Allison had given Jean pointers on questions that she could ask Marian at the bridal boutique.

"I have become more used, to introducing myself. I have never created, and sewn anything for sale in the past. I know things will continue, to go well".

After Jean and Allison finished working, and going over some details, they had a better idea of the way, the design would look.

"I learned a lot of details from Sara. I' am unable to remember all the details we went through. Lowell has given me his opinions, on designs he has seen in the past".

Jean had been able to keep her life organized, despite the time she was spending on her designs. She wanted her life to remain organized.

Allison had a long day. She had begun with a meeting, and then she had a photo shoot for, several, hours. Allison had not imagined that she would be sewing, that day.

Lynn had been focused, at completing her work.

Allison read the newspaper earlier. The headline referred to a car accident that occurred, the day before. There were some injuries. The injuries would make two people remain, in the hospital. Allison imagined how difficult the situation, must have been.

Allison thought of the work, that she had done, with Floyd. He had been nice, and genuine. Allison meant to ask him how long the advertisement would run. She wanted to know, when it was supposed, to begin. It would take time for the agency to prepare the details. The agency was responding to her slowly, at this time. Allison knew that they had a lot of people involved in preparing, the advertisement. The agency, as well as the other people involved, had other projects to complete. Having the photos would assist her to keep track of the projects she has done.

Allison noticed that Lynn had drifted off to sleep. She had not awakened, after, several, moments. At least Lynn had not had to go to school, that next day. She would have the day off. Lynn planned to spend the time with Sammy. She had become used to having a two day weekend. Lynn sometimes slept longer, on Saturday mornings.

Sammy had been resting.

Allison met Floyd the next morning. He invited her to have coffee with him. They were supposed to discuss photos, and choose two, that would go inside the advertisement.

Floyd sat two portfolios on the table, as they drank coffee. He explained the terms of the contract. Floyd told Allison, the company would run the advertisement for six months.

"Allison, the agency does not want you to complete any similar advertisements for a while. They would not want things to become confusing for the agencies".

Floyd had been able to convince the agency, to use a photo with Allison wearing the gown that Jean created.

Allison had been glad. She wanted to let Jean know.

Allison excused herself. She found a phone.

Allison called Jean.

Jean had been glad to hear about the news.

"Allison, I' am glad, that they decided to use my gown. They decided quickly. I have been designing clothes for a long time. I' am glad, that they came to an agreement on what designs they were looking to use".

"You create wonderful designs Jean".

Allison stayed on the phone for, several, additional minutes. She told Jean, that she would talk with her later.

Jean told Allison, that she would wait to talk with her later.

An hour after the meeting ended, Allison returned home.

When Allison arrived home, Jean had been working on the same design. The gown had been red. Jean drew an outline for the design a while ago. She told Allison, that she originally began, with, several, different patterns. Jean wanted to design the gown with the pattern that looked the best. She enjoyed using her creativity. That assisted her to enjoy designing.

"In another month the gown would be completed. I was on the phone part of the day, with three boutiques that are interested in buying gowns. They wanted to receive information on, several, of my designs. The boutiques enjoyed working with designers they were unfamiliar with".

Jean had been trying to complete some work. Things were becoming difficult. Jean had been working on the area around the waist. She knew that it was more of a challenge to work in that area, but thought that she would be able to manage.

Allison watched Jean for a moment. She poured them a cup of coffee.

Jean appreciated the assistance Allison was giving her.

Jean had been busy working. She said that Lynn arrived to her home by midmorning. Lynn assisted Jean, by drawing, several, sketches of possible future designs. Jean had not taken a break throughout the day.

Lynn managed to keep herself busy, when she began drawing.

Allison and Jean had been in the kitchen working. Allison could tell that Jean wanted to concentrate on the details of her gown. After they finished sewing the sides of the gown, Allison and Jean worked a while on the sequins on the front of the gown.

Lynn told Allison that she had been restless.

Allison and Lynn walked home. That way Jean could finish more of her work.

Lynn had gone inside her room to read, before she decided to go to bed.

Allison had, several, meetings that were scheduled. The prospective clients for Dellkes Realty were supposed to meet her at the office. Allison hoped that the prospective clients, decided to complete their real estate contracts with Delkes Realty. She had never met them in the past. The prospective clients called the office, and stated they had been interested in new properties. Allison scheduled the meetings, so they could become familiar with the office. She planned to keep the realtors in the office informed about the contracts for the prospective clients.

Mark was home with his family.

When Allison thought, that the client was not going to come to the office, she looked through, several, files.

Her desk phone began ringing.

Allison answered the phone.

The client was on the other end of the phone.

Allison wondered why the client had not come to the meeting.

The client explained that he had been running late, because of a business meeting. He was hoping that Allison and he could have a conference by phone. The client had not thought that it would take long, since he had already met with the selling realtor.

Allison needed to give the client, an idea of the structure of the loan. She told him, that she would be able to get the information to him. Allison asked the client, several, more questions about his other mortgage.

Allison and the gentleman went through more of their conference. It had taken them a while. The gentleman had been the owner of a restaurant located in the city. Allison and the gentleman finished the details.

Allison wanted the gentleman to be able to get back to his restaurant. He had to attend to his establishment.

The gentleman wanted the opportunity to purchase a different house. He lived at the home for, several, years, before his wife died. He had not wanted to live in the home anymore.

Allison reminded the gentleman, that all the details were stated in his contract. The gentleman was grateful, that Allison had been willing to have a conference by phone.

The gentleman reminded Allison, that she could stop by the restaurant whenever she wanted. He thought that she would enjoy the menu.

"It took me, several, years to organize the menu. So far the restaurant has been worth the investment. I have managed to generate enough business".

The gentleman told Allison that he would call the office, if he had any additional questions.

When Allison finished the conference with the gentleman, her office phone rang, several, minutes later.

Mark invited her, to see the baby that evening.

Allison agreed.

Allison thought that Lynn may want to come.

Mark had been looking forward to Allison and Lynn visiting.

"When Lynn and you come to visit, we will not have anything extravagant planned. Gillian is still recuperating from the birth. She came home weeks ago. Anne has grown since, she left the hospital".

Mark had not wanted to have a busy schedule for a while. Especially, since Gillian and Mark, thought there might be complications from the birth.

Allison prepared to leave the office. She had gone toward home. Allison called Jean, before she left the office, to let Lynn know of the plans.

Lynn wore a party dress.

Allison drove twenty minutes.

Allison and Lynn arrived to the home of Mark and Gillian.

Mark and Gillian greeted Allison and Lynn. Anne had been wearing a dress. Gillian held her in her arms.

Lynn initially was shy. She responded with a smile. Lynn had never met Mark before. She had not met Anne.

Allison stood next to Gillian. She handed Anne to Allison.

Allison could remember when she had taken off work when Lynn had been born. It was over a month. At the time, she had been transferring out of her career in real estate property. Allison had to show, several, real estate properties to prospective clients. Edgar took care of Lynn for, several, hours, once Allison had gone to work.

Everyone sat in the dining room. Mark found a red wine. He found juice for Lynn.

Lynn drank her juice, as the adults talked.

Mark asked Allison about the office.

Allison told Mark that things had been there usual. She told him about her phone conference with a recent buyer. The details had taken a while, but she had gotten through it. Allison was sure that the real estate contract would be completed soon.

Allison had not completed any loans in two days.

Mark told Allison that his parents had taken the train home. His parents would stay home for, several, days, but planned to return soon. Gillian and he would return to work at their offices.

"Allison I must say, that I do miss working inside the office. I assume that I must have, several, messages, within the past, several, weeks. I have tried to complete some work at home. This office does not have all the same materials".

Mark was glad that he was able to accomplish some work at home. He remained silent for, several, moments.

Gillian offered everyone, something else.

Lynn had been enjoying her time. Lynn had not minded being the only child around adults. She had been spending time drawing, and playing Frisbee with Sammy and Zealand lately. Lynn made plans to go to an acquaintance home the following day.

Mark and Gillian had been anxious for the baby to come. Once Anne had been born, they had been staying up at night with her. Similar to when David was born.

"David had been anxious for, several, months. We continued to stay up with him. He would always forget why he had been upset".

Several, minutes later, David had awoken. He had come into the dining room. David apologized for leaving his room. He had been shy.

Gillian stood up and took David's hand. She assured him, that he would be able to return to sleep.

Gillian excused David and she, and promised that she would return.

Mark mentioned to Allison, that before the holidays, Gillian and he planned to give David a birthday party.

"You are welcome to come with Lynn. We plan, to have, several, relatives at the party. Gillian's sister plans to come into town for, several, days. I think she will be completing some work".

Allison told Mark, that Lynn, and she would come to the party. She had not had any other plans, before the holidays. Allison thought that it would be a good way, to celebrate the holiday season.

Gillian returned to the room, and reminded everyone, that David had school the next day.

Mark told his wife, that Allison and Lynn planned to come to the birthday party for David.

Gillian mentioned that there would be, several, family, and acquaintances at the birthday party.

"David has not had as many people around him, for his birthday".

Mark decided to show Allison, some notes on details of a house he had been trying, to sell.

"I think that, I will be able to have you work on, the loan soon".

Allison looked at the notes, and realized how long it had been taking to sell the house. The family had been trying to sell the house, for three months. It had not received a lot of interest. Mark had been assisting a recent client that was interested, in the house.

"Things will be clearer, in, several, days. At this time, I' am unable to get the client to make a final decision. The client mentioned that they wanted to talk, with relatives. They would contact me after the holidays. Allison, I assume, that they will decide, that they want to sign the documents, for the house".

"I should be used to not being able to finalize, all the details right away. That is a concern with real estate sells. The constant changes can make things difficult, to understand".

Mark asked Lynn questions, about Sammy.

Lynn reminded Mark, that the dog was an Australian Terrier. She was barely larger than Zealand. Lynn told Mark, that Zealand had been her neighbor's dog. She had been eager to talk about Jean, and Zealand.

After Lynn finished eating, she reminded Mark of the new class pet. Lynn mentioned that the class hamsters, will be able to go on class trips.

Mark enjoyed talking to Lynn, about her ideas about school.

"Lynn, you are having a great time at school. You are learning a lot".

Lynn agreed with Mark.

Lynn told Mark, that the class hamster was growing.

The conversation Mark was having with Lynn, ended when Lynn thought about the time. She reminded Allison, that she had to go to class the next day.

Allison knew that Lynn had a long day.

Allison mentioned to Mark and Gillian that Lynn and she needed to leave, because the time had been late.

Allison did not have any early meetings, but she planned to bring Lynn to school.

David had fallen to sleep. He had been younger than Lynn. David would begin regular school age classes, the following fall.

Lynn had enjoyed her time visiting Mark, Gillian, and David. She wondered if they could visit the family more often.

"It would be difficult, Allison told her. They have two children, and will need to spend time with them. Anne is a baby. When they do invite us to visit, then we will go".

Lynn was content with this answer. She remained quiet, until they arrived home.

Allison found a bouquet of flowers with a note from Jean.

Jean thanked Allison for assisting her with the two gowns.

Allison thought it was a beautiful gesture.

As Allison and Lynn walked into the dining room, the phone began ringing.

Hansen had been on the other end.

Hansen told Allison, that he talked with a gentleman from a popular magazine, and he wanted to have her in one of their advertisements. It involved a one time work. Allison would need to call the gentleman the next day.

Allison had worked on, several, photo shoots at a time.

"It is nice that you are able to do a lot of work in town. It is nice that you do not have to travel far to work. You have time to decide, if you want to complete the photo shoot".

Allison told Hansen, that she would meet the photographer at his studio. She had been unsure of what she needed to bring.

Hansen told Allison, the photo shoot would be great for her, before ending the conversation. It had been a long day for him. He wanted to give her the information.

Hansen told Allison, that she would receive the details of the photo shoot.

Allison was glad to be able to do modeling work. She had not expected the call. Allison had been spending some time working, since she began her new career.

When Allison and Hansen ended their conversation, she called Lowell.

Lowell had been glad for Allison. He told her about a photo shoot, that he had earlier that day. It lasted for two hours.

"I went into the city. There was a model that planned to be in the city for a week. She had planned to be part of, several, photo shoots. Her agency would decide on which photos they plan to use. They are working with three different experienced photographers, and will probably look through about fifty photos. They are going to use three for the advertisement".

"Models gain, a lot, of exposure".

Allison understood more about modeling and photography, than she had in the past. She liked the idea of starting small, and gaining more exposure.

Lowell mentioned that he would be going into the city to complete another photo shoot. He wanted to buy some additional camera equipment.

"Being a photographer can be a busy career. Depending on your type of photography, it can be a lot to remember the details of a photo shoot. It is important to keep track of the appointment times, and the place that you are scheduled to be at. The photo shoot could involve the use of different equipment. When the opportunity is first introduced, as a photographer, you are given the information of what you are expected to do".

Lowell was grateful about his career.

"Allison, I need to be prepared for tomorrow. The agency is requesting certain types of images. They want, several, different backgrounds".

Allison wished Lowell luck with the photo shoot.

Lynn told Allison that she had a long day.

When Lynn laid her head down, she had fallen asleep.

Allison finished reading the newspaper.

Allison had not received any messages. She had not expected to see Mark, inside the office. Mark told Allison, that he would not be at work, for another, several, days.

"Allison, I came to work, because a client wants to sign documents, for his house. I mentioned this to you, the other evening. Anyway, we are planning to meet in two hours. At least I know the meeting will go well. After he officially tells me, that he wants to sign the documents for the house, then I will call you".

Allison reminded Mark, that she planned to leave the office. She would check her messages. If he called, she would return his call.

Allison reminded Mark, that she had a photo shoot, that she had to complete. She would try to complete it, within, several, hours. The schedule for the photo shoot was unpredictable. Allison had not wanted to inconvenience the photographer, by rescheduling. He may have other obligations.

Allison had not met the photographer. His name was Eric. They talked briefly on the phone.

Allison told Mark, that she was confident the client would complete the real estate documents, with Delkes Realty.

"Allison, I hope that you do well at your photo shoot. I know that you have other obligations that you have to complete, besides here inside the office".

When Allison arrived to the photo shoot, the equipment had to be set up.

"A colleague allowed me to borrow his studio. I was told of your career, and that you most likely would not have the time to come into the city. I thought that I would come into town, instead".

Allison told Eric, that she appreciated, that he decided to complete the photo shoot inside the town.

Eric began setting up his equipment.

From what Allison could remember, Eric had been a photographer for over twenty years. He sensed, what she must have been thinking, and lifted his right eye brow. Everything had been prepared, to complete the photo shoot.

After the work had been completed, Eric complemented Allison on the photo shoot. He told her that the photos would come out well. If anything changed, Eric would let Allison know. He told her, that he planned to bring them directly to the persons involved with the advertisement. When Eric and Allison finished their conference, Allison thanked Eric, and left. She wanted to go to the office in case Mark called.

When Allison arrived inside the office, Mary gave her a message from Mark.

"He said that he needed your assistance to process a loan. He would not be able to complete the documents without it".

Allison called the phone number that Mark left. It was to the house of the client. Allison felt bad for making them wait. She answered, several, of the financial questions, and Mark told her that he would return the documents to the office, once the documents were signed.

The gentleman agreed to the information Allison gave him.

Allison decided that she would visit the business meeting.

The traffic was uncongested, and Allison drove through the streets, to the nearby area of town. The house was initially difficult to find. Most of the clients that Mark assisted recently were in the nearby area.

Allison found the two gentlemen inside the kitchen. They had been drinking a cup of coffee.

Mark was glad to see her.

"We are almost ready to conclude the meeting".

Mark handed Allison the documents to look over. When she finished looking over the documents, Allison handed the documents to the gentleman, so he could add additional information.

The gentleman introduced himself as Ivan. He offered Allison, a cup of coffee.

Allison had not planned to stay at the meeting long. She mentioned that she would be driving home soon.

He understood, and told her maybe next time, they could talk longer.

Mark began to explain to Ivan, the details of the contract. Allison listened, as the gentlemen talked through, their meeting.

Allison looked around the kitchen. She noticed the details of the design. Things were going well with, the meeting. Allison waited, to make sure there would not be any additional questions. Mark or Ivan had not had any additional questions. Allison left, and drove home, to Lynn.

Jean noticed Allison, as she came into the drive. She had been throwing Frisbee, with Zealand.

"I have some great news! I received a call from a woman, by the name of Joan. She is going to an event that will be, with, several, models. She asked me if I would introduce two of my gowns".

"Joan noticed in an advertisement, that you were wearing, one of my designs. They want to use, several, of my gowns, in an event. They also want designs, by, several, other designers'. They will need to be ready in two months. I told Joan, that I would be able to manage that. She wants me to create, two original gowns".

Allison had been glad for Jean.

Allison and Jean went inside.

Allison began looking at, several, outlines that Jean, had drawn. Jean managed to complete them, within, several, hours. Jean had design materials that were, sprawled out.

"Using my new sewing machine will allow me to finish, the gowns sooner".

Jean began to gather some materials, as Allison and she began to work. After, several, minutes, Jean, and Allison were sewing together fabrics, for a gown.

"It will not be completed today, but at least we could have a start".

Allison had not wanted to break the concentration, by talking about her photo shoot, that day.

"Allison, I' am not completely aware of all the details. At least I created an idea, of what Joan wants".

"Joan said that she had been looking for a designer similar to me. She said that she wanted someone that would add something original.

Joan wanted each gown to have some original quality. Joan mentioned that, several, designers she talked with, were unable to assist her. They had other obligations at this time. Joan had been glad that I was able to feature some designs in her fashion event. That was the extent of our initial conversation".

Jean and Allison continued to work.

Lynn had been inside the home with Jean and Allison. She decided to stay inside, and draw, after she finished her assignments for class. Lynn worked, as Allison and Jean continued to work on the designs. Lynn did not want to disturb them.

Jean told Allison that she had been working most of the day on the designs. Lynn and she had been having a great time, as they put together the designs.

Jean, Allison, and Lynn ate a late dinner.

"I knew that it would take me a while to work on the gown. I would like to have additional people assist me with creating my designs".

They remained at the table.

Lynn was relieved that the young boy in the class began to behave. She heard him apologize to Ms. Rosner. When her teacher ended class two days ago, the young boy assisted her to reorganize some things in the classroom. The class hamster had not been feeling well.

"Hopefully he will be fine soon".

Allison told Jean and Lynn about the photo shoot. Everyone enjoyed the conversation. Allison had not wanted her daughter to worry about anything she had not needed to.

Lynn looked as if she had a long day. Things had been moving fast for her. Her school year was becoming more challenging.

"We have the day after the holiday off".

Lynn mentioned that it would be nice to visit Mark, Gillian, and both their children for the holidays.

Allison told Lynn that she would have to ask them.

That next morning, was Lynn's last day of school, before the holiday. Ms. Rosner had an in class project, for the class.

Lynn was up early, that next morning.

Allison drove Lynn to school.

Lynn had other things on her mind.

Allison asked Lynn, what she had been thinking. She thought that maybe it had to do, with the class project, that day. Allison knew that, Lynn would figure through what she had been thinking about. Lynn was a determined person.

Lynn began to talk.

Lynn told Allison, that she had always enjoyed the class projects. Lynn was unsure, if the class would receive additional class work, that day, because of the project, the class would be working on. Lynn had been fine, with the change.

Allison had not planned on going inside the office, that day. Instead, she would complete work around the home. Allison planned to take care of some errands. Later that afternoon, she had planned to complete another photo shoot with a photographer. Afterwards, Allison planned to visit, several, stores in order to gain other materials that Jean, and she would need in order, to complete a gown.

Jean knew that she wanted a lot of detail, in the upcoming design. Jean insisted, on expanding, on the design. She wanted to add sequins in several, areas in the front, and back of the gown. It would be cream. Jean mentioned in the past, that it had been one of her favorite colors, in a gown.

Allison and Jean worked, for a while.

Sammy and Zealand had been resting in the living room.

Jean and Allison drank warmed tea, as they began, to sew a gown.

"I remember watching my mother sew".

Allison had been glad that she was able to assist Jean.

"If you would have asked me a while ago I would not have thought I wanted to begin designing again. I may have decided to do something different. For the longest time I had sewn for my family and acquaintances".

Jean asked Allison about Sara, and her design business.

Allison told Jean that she recently talked with Sara.

"Sara was keeping her designing business going. She had not wanted to change her business plan. Sara enjoyed being in contact with individuals about her gowns. I' am sure that she is selling some of the gowns at her boutique. Sara's gowns have been a focus at her boutique. She did mention to me that she would like to do more events. Sara has become used to them".

Allison enjoyed the way that the gown was coming together. Outside of her photo shoots, Allison could not remember a time that she needed to wear an elaborate gown. She had never worn anything as detailed as the designs Jean and she were creating. Allison recalled, several, years ago, when she wore a beautiful gown to a banquet for real estate. Sara made the gown. She had done a great job, and allowed Allison to keep it.

Sammy had begun barking, and looking through the window. It had become late in the afternoon. Sammy looked as if she were ready to run.

Lynn had come inside the home.

"I had not heard any noise from inside our home, so I came here. You forgot to pick me up from school. I' am fine. I was able to get a ride from another parent. I was waiting for half an hour. I went to the office, and called our home, and had not received an answer".

Allison apologized to her daughter.

Jean and she had been working, and she had not noticed the time. Allison meant to leave over an hour ago.

"Lynn, I have been trying to do, several, things at once".

Lynn began giving Zealand and Sammy attention. They followed her in another room. She checked their water bowls. Lynn changed the water bowls of Zealand and Sammy.

Lynn cleared their water bowls when they were finished. She had taken Zealand and Sammy outside to play Frisbee.

Lynn must have forgotten about the photo shoot Allison had completed that day. She usually wanted to ask questions. Allison had been waiting for Lynn to ask her about the photo shoot.

Jean, Allison, and Lynn talked more, before Jean and Allison stopped working.

Lynn called to Sammy as she led her outside. Sammy and she walked home.

Allison wanted to assist Jean with the cleaning of their work. When they finished, she walked home by herself.

Lynn had been inside the kitchen, giving Sammy a bowl of water. She must have been thirsty, and finished the last of it.

"I knew that Sammy had been thirsty. Now I' am unsure of where her food had been moved to".

Allison had apologized, and said that she had forgotten to buy more food after she fed her that afternoon.

"We will need to go to the store, and buy more food for Sammy".

Allison, and Lynn had gotten into the car, and Allison drove to the local store.

The store had not been crowded. Allison and Lynn found what they were looking for.

Allison and Lynn arrived home.

Lynn decided to go to bed.

The next morning, Gillian called to wish everyone a great holiday. She told Allison, that the family planned on having relatives from the city visit throughout the day. Allison and Lynn should try, and reschedule their visit. The relatives planned to visit, because of the new baby. They had not had a definite time.

Allison told Gillian, that Lynn would understand, because they had not had any definite plans to visit the family.

Jean invited Allison, and Lynn, to bring Sammy over to visit Zealand, and she. They were supposed to meet her at noon.

There had been announcements, that there would be live events in the area.

Allison and Lynn had not planned to attend any of the events. The past three years, Allison could remember them going.

Lynn had been disappointed, because for the holiday she thought there would be snow.

Allison would have liked for it to snow, as well. She told Lynn, that it may snow within the next, several, weeks. It will continue to remain clear throughout that day.

Lynn talked with Edgar. He wished everyone a great holiday.

Afterward, Lynn assisted Allison with finding the Christmas decorations. They would soon begin to set up their decorations.

Later, they had been ready to visit Jean.

When Allison and Lynn arrived to the door, she could hear Zealand barking.

Jean smiled when she noticed them.

"You would think that I would choose not to work on the holiday. I decided to awake, and complete some work, on my latest design".

Jean told Allison, and Lynn, that she had not had a chance to prepare the dinner.

Jean mentioned, several, days ago, that her family would not be able, to come to visit. They had obligations, at work.

Everyone agreed that they had plenty of choices, at dinner. Lynn had specifically enjoyed the tea that was prepared. They planned to eat within two hours. Lynn continued to keep Zealand, and Sammy entertained.

For an hour, Allison, and Jean worked, on a gown.

Afterward, Jean, and Lynn sat down at a table in the dining room, and began to play a board game. The game had been recently bought.

After they played the game, Jean told Lynn, that she could have it. Lynn appreciated the gift.

An hour later, everyone finished eating.

Jean and Allison talked about the work, at the real estate office.

Allison told Jean, about a recent client. The loan had been approved, within a day.

After, Jean, and Allison finished talking, Allison brought the dishes, to the sink. After Allison finished cleaning, she told Jean, that she would see her, the next day.

Sammy reluctantly, followed behind Allison, and Lynn. It had been a similar scene, as in the past.

Lynn mentioned that she felt bad, that Sammy was unable to play with Zealand anymore, that day.

At home, Sammy went directly, to her water bowl.

When Sammy finished drinking water, she walked into the other room. Sammy was content.

Lynn had been drawing. Allison and Lynn enjoyed, their time together.

Allison and Lynn sorted through the Christmas decorations.

Allison told Lynn, that they would wait until tomorrow, to think about the tree.

Lynn agreed.

Lynn said that they would have more time, to set up the decorations.

That day, Jean had appreciated the company. She even sketched, several, possible future designs.

Allison had been in the middle of her thoughts, when Lowell called.

Lowell was glad to hear, the voice of Allison.

"Allison, I had not talked to you in, several, days. I know that you had plans with colleagues".

Allison reminded Lowell, that her plans had changed. Gillian mentioned that relatives would be visiting. They wanted to see Anne.

"It worked out fine, because we visited with Jean. Her plans had changed. In fact, we spent time working on a gown. It took us a while, to get the design started".

"I' am glad, that you were able to enjoy, the holiday. I went into the city to complete some work. There is an agency that had been waiting on some photos that I needed to create. I delivered their photos, to them. I drove to a restaurant, and ate lunch. When I arrived home, I decided to call you. I knew that you would not mind being called on a holiday. I thought maybe you, had not had any appointments. Too bad, I could not say the same. I' am always busy, as a photographer. I do not get much time off. I enjoy being, a photographer".

Allison invited Lowell over for coffee. They had not talked in nearly a week. Allison had been waiting for him, when he arrived.

Lowell had been glad to see Allison. She poured them a cup of coffee. They sat inside the kitchen, and he had been trying to think through a situation. He continued to talk to Allison, about his day. He had shown her, several, photos, of the photo shoot.

"Allison, we have a lot in common. That is why I think we, are close acquaintances. Lately, I have been talking with you, more than anyone else I know".

Lowell wanted to talk with Allison, about the agency.

Allison told Lowell, that Hansen had been kind. The agency has been doing well, at getting her involved, in photo shoots.

Lowell told Allison that, several, people at the photo shoot were individuals he has worked with in the past.

Lowell and Allison finished their coffee.

Lynn had gone to bed moments before. Allison had not wanted to disturb her.

Ice was starting to form on the window sills, from the cold air outside. The night temperature changed drastically, during the winter months.

"Allison, you have remained a good acquaintance".

Lowell told Allison that he had talked with Daniel. He told Lowell everyone was doing fine. They had not talked as often as they used to. Daniel and Amy made plans for their families to visit in December.

"Maybe if you would like, we could have a dinner at my home".

Lowell agreed.

Lowell thought dinner with Allison and Lynn would be a great idea.

"At least you would be with Lynn, Sammy, and me".

Lowell began to look forward to the dinner. He had a lot to say that evening.

Allison continued to listen to what Lowell was saying.

Lowell reminded Allison that he had gone through a long day. He suggested that Allison should rest. She had a photo shoot that next day.

"The agency has been giving you a lot of work. They want to make sure that you receive plenty of exposure. They have become a good source for you. I think that you will continue to be part of some popular print advertisements".

An hour later, Lowell left.

Allison had been downstairs alone. Sammy walked toward her. She sensed that Allison had a long day. Allison ruffled the dog, before she went upstairs to her room.

It was the first time that Lynn had come on a photo shoot with Allison. She had a no nonsense attitude.

The photographer knew who Lynn was. He approached her, and shook her hand. He came over to Allison, and did the same.

"I' am familiar with your photos. We have a lot of work ahead of us today".

Allison was glad that Lynn and she were spending the day together. She had not known how long the photo shoot would take.

The photographer told Allison the details of the photo shoot.

Lynn began wandering around the building.

Lynn returned to the area of the photo shoot.

Lynn approached her mother and the photographer.

Allison spoke.

"We took, several, photos".

Allison had been wearing makeup. It took a while to apply.

Lynn remained quiet, as Allison discussed the photo shoot with the photographer.

The gentleman told Allison, when she would be able to contact the office about the photos.

"The agency will receive copies in, several, days. They will give you any additional information that you need. I know that you are used to hearing that".

The photographer gave Allison and Lynn another handshake, before they left. Things had gone well during the photo shoot.

Allison and Lynn went to lunch at a nearby restaurant. The restaurant had not been crowded. Allison and Lynn arrived, directly after the lunch crowd. Lynn added a salad with her lunch. Allison had done the same.

Allison noticed Edgar come inside the restaurant.

Edgar noticed Allison, and Lynn. He walked toward them, and kissed Lynn on the head.

"I was told from a source, that you were here".

Edgar explained that he had known Allison had begun modeling. He told her, that Hansen told him, that Allison and Lynn were at the restaurant.

"I know that I do not get a chance to spend as much time, with Lynn or you, but I have taken a small break, from the peace organization. I decided to rent a house in town. I plan to be there for, several, weeks. Afterwards, I plan to buy a house".

Lynn was happy about this news.

Allison knew, that Lynn had been thinking that her parents would become remarried, to each other.

Lynn asked Edgar, about the recent details, of his life.

Edgar explained that he no longer was dating the woman, in the peace organization.

Lynn mentioned to Edgar, that she hoped, it was not, because of her.

Edgar told Lynn, that she had not been the reason, they were not dating.

"We had been analyzing our relationship for, several, months. We realized our relationship was not the best thing for us".

Edgar asked Allison, if she had begun, dating anyone.

Allison shook her head, in an answer of, no.

Allison told Edgar, that she had been assisting Jean. She told him, that she had been working inside the office. Allison reminded Edgar, that she had been completing, several, photo shoots.

"Jean has decided to continue her career, as a designer. I have been assisting her with sewing her designs".

"Allison, I was hoping that we could become acquaintances, again. It has been a while, since we last talked. I know that we have changed, and now live separate lives. Maybe we could communicate, more, in the future".

Allison knew that Edgar had been trying to be more involved in how Lynn and she were living their lives.

Edgar continued to talk with his daughter.

Edgar brought a camera with him, and wanted to take photos. Lynn was smiling in the photos. She was glad to be able to have this time with her father. The photos looked, as if Edgar, Allison, and Lynn were used to taking photos together. They were glad to be together.

An hour later, Edgar, Allison, and Lynn left the restaurant. Allison and Lynn had gone their separate way from Edgar. He promised Allison and Lynn that he would call them soon.

Lynn had been glad to see Edgar.

Allison had known that things would go well for Edgar. She had not wanted to reestablish an intimate relationship with him. Allison knew that Edgar would want to make things similar to the way they had been, when Lynn was younger.

Allison and Lynn walked to their car.

As they entered the car, Lynn wanted to ask Allison about her parents dating again. Lynn knew, that she would not receive the answer she was looking for then.

Lynn asked Allison about her birthday party. She told Allison, that she wanted a dinner party, for her birthday.

Allison told Lynn, that it was her decision.

Plans were made for the party to be the following week. Allison had an idea of what she wanted to get her daughter for her birthday. There was a new art book that she wanted. Allison noticed a beautiful gold necklace with a single diamond. Allison thought these would be the best things for Lynn.

On the way home, Allison and Lynn stopped by a boutique. Lynn found a dress that she would wear to the dinner. The dress was a pale blue. Lynn planned to wear it also to the Christmas dinner.

An hour later, Allison and Lynn arrived home.

Lynn told Allison, that it was nice that there will be, several, close people, at the party.

Allison and Lynn prepared dinner. It had not taken them long to finish. Lynn became quiet.

Allison asked Lynn, if there was anything on her mind.

Lynn asked Allison, if Edgar could come to her birthday party, since he had planned to be in town.

Allison agreed.

Allison told Lynn, that it would be fine with her.

Allison and Lynn sat together, and completed their dinner. They made plans to go out the next day, and complete some shopping.

Allison had been glad, that Lynn wanted to have a dinner party for her birthday. Usually children her age wanted to play with acquaintances. Lynn in many ways reminded Allison, when she had been her age.

When Lynn finished eating, she left Allison to clean the kitchen. She wanted to draw.

Lynn had come into the kitchen, and asked the opinion of Allison. She had drawn an outdoor scene. It consisted of, several, different combinations of colors.

Lynn had not remembered until later, that she had not completed the assignment for class. Lynn began to complete the assignment.

Allison wondered what Lynn would choose to do as a career, when she became older.

Sammy was lying next to Lynn, as she sat at the dining room table. She had been an older dog. Lately, Sammy had become more reclusive at home. She enjoyed being around Zealand. It had almost been time for Sammy to visit Joyce Eagleston.

An hour later, Allison combed through Sammy's hair.

Lynn had been sleeping. She planned to enjoy her weekend off from school.

Allison thought it would be a good idea to call Edgar, and remind him of the dinner party. Allison knew that he would want to attend.

Edgar had not intended to keep Allison in a long conversation. He mentioned that he had still been adjusting to his new lifestyle. Edgar was living alone. He planned to complete more work with the peace organization.

When they talked, Edgar reminded Allison, how different it was for him, after his relationship ended. Edgar and the woman had been spending a lot of time together. She wanted things to progress in their relationship, and they continue their work with the peace organization. Edgar told Allison, that most people joined the peace organization for, several, years.

"I do feel bad that things had to change. Maybe one day, I will decide to remarry. At this time, I' am unsure if I will make that decision".

Edgar told Allison that before the woman, and he had stopped dating, that it felt as if they had already been married.

"I think this is a good time, for me to do more things, with Lynn. She is young. She is going through school".

Allison agreed with Edgar.

Allison was glad, that Edgar was able to spend more time with Lynn.

"Lynn has told me, that, she would like to do more things with you".

"We have plenty of activities that we can, do together".

Edgar remained quiet. He expected Allison to say something else.

Allison told Edgar, about their neighbor. Jean had become an acquaintance, toward Allison, and Lynn.

"She tries to visit the town she was born in, when she is able to. Jean is working on designs, to her gowns. They are coming along, great".

"Somehow, we will manage to make sure Lynn, is taken care of for the next, several, years".

Allison told Edgar, that she planned to buy a cake, for the dinner party. She had not wanted Lynn to know about the cake. Allison would not be able to make the cake, at home.

Allison explained to Edgar, that it would be his opportunity to meet Mark, and his family. Jean also planned to be at the dinner.

"Allison, there have not been any birthdays, that I had not spent with Lynn. I managed to be around her, at the time. I' am glad, that she wants me at the dinner".

Allison felt bad, that Edgar continued to think about the busy lifestyle that he led in the past. Edgar and Lynn would talk in, several, days. Edgar asked Allison to tell him about the things, that Lynn liked. He asked, if she had any other hobbies, besides drawing.

Allison told Edgar, that Lynn recently began to assist in taking care of Sammy.

Edgar had been glad, that Lynn spent time, with Sammy.

Allison began to talk about real estate. Allison told Edgar about a recent client that had been looking for a house for, a while. The gentleman had not decided on the amount, that he wanted to pay toward the house. The office had not wanted to rush the sell. They would wait, until he made, his decision.

Edgar thought that it sounded to be a stressful real estate sell. Allison and he ended their phone conversation.

Allison had, several, meetings, that next day. She planned to leave the office early. Allison wanted to buy Lynn, several, books, and wanted to buy Lynn another dress, for her birthday dinner. She planned to pick Lynn up, from school.

Allison found the stores that she had been looking for. She bought a dress for Lynn. A gentleman at the store assisted her to make sure, it was the correct size.

Allison had arrived home.

Allison prepared the home, for the dinner party. There had been, several, vases that contained flowers on the table. The table also consisted of place settings. Allison wanted to create a neutral atmosphere for younger and older adults. She knew Lynn would appreciate the neutral atmosphere.

Jean had been at home working. She was finishing her last gown that week, for the fashion event that she was part of.

"The individuals in charge of the event are expecting the gowns soon".

Jean planned to deliver the gowns by the end of the following week. The individuals in charge of the event would be glad to have the gowns.

Allison noticed that the home was quiet. Jean had been inside. Allison continued to think about Jean, as she left home. The skies were becoming darker. Allison left the home, to pick Lynn up from school.

Allison arrived to the school, and Lynn had been waiting for her. Lynn had gotten inside the car.

"I had not wanted you to have to look for me. I waited here. I know that we need to arrive home, for the dinner party. I feel bad, that my acquaintances from class are unable to attend. I do think, they would have enjoyed being, at the dinner".

Allison and Lynn talked about the latest details, on the class pet.

"Our hamster is a lot of fun. He moves around a lot. I do not think that he will grow to be much bigger".

Allison enjoyed their conversations. After they talked about the class pet, Lynn had been curious about Mark, and his family.

Allison reminded Lynn, that she had not talked to them, in, several, days. They were adjusting their work schedules, because they were taking care of Anne. She continued to enjoy her time with her parents, during the day.

"Mark's parents had agreed for, several, weeks, to assist them with the new baby. Ginger and Marin live outside the city".

Lynn was glad, that everyone was doing well.

Allison and Lynn arrived home. Lynn found, that everything had been arranged for the dinner party. She found her dress, and admired the design. She was happy to receive two new dresses, in a short time period.

Lynn wore the new dress. She planned to wait, to open the remaining gifts. Lynn wanted to open her gifts, once everyone arrived.

Jean had been the first to arrive to the dinner party. She arrived with Zealand. He gave the impression, as if he had known they were, celebrating, Lynn's birthday. Zealand walked toward Lynn, and barked. Jean handed Lynn a wrapped box, and another wrapped item. Lynn put them away, once Zealand remained calm.

Allison, Jean, and Lynn sat down, and waited for the other guests to arrive.

Hansen had come to the dinner.

Mark had come with Gillian, and their two children.

Everyone was impressed by the design of the room. There had been a fire in the fireplace.

Edgar arrived last, to the dinner party.

Everyone continued eating.

After they ate, everyone continued to stay. Sammy and Zealand began to watch everyone. Allison and Lynn continued to talk with everyone. Edgar talked of the places he had visited, with the peace organization.

Lynn said that she had been exhausted, after the long evening. She had decided to go to bed.

Lynn left Allison, and Edgar.

Allison and Edgar talked.

Allison and Edgar sat across from each other at the table. He mentioned, that he thought, they should remain acquaintances. Edgar had not talked to Allison in, several, days. He had not wanted things between them to be intimidating. Edgar remained concerned for Lynn. Allison appreciated that, as they talked. She was becoming familiar with Edgar again. They had not held any animosity toward each other.

"Allison, I' am glad for your success with raising Lynn. I know, that you have her most of the time".

Allison accepted his complement. Edgar had worn black slacks, and a gray sweater.

"Allison, I think, that I may have had too much going on, in the past".

Edgar noticed Lynn's drawings and paintings around the home.

Allison thought of those times that she would arrive home from the office after showing properties. Selling properties sometimes developed complications.

"I made things complicated for myself".

Allison had not known what Edgar expected of her now. They sat for a while.

Sara called, and wanted to give Allison updated news. She had sold a gown, and needed to make, several, more.

"Some of my designs were featured in the local newspaper. The one thing I can do is, allow for myself, to have more exposure, and have quantities at some of the boutiques. You are a close acquaintance Allison. I do appreciate all of your support. Maybe we will work together in the future".

Allison gave Sara the details of her next photo shoot.

"Allison, I' am glad that you are able to meet with photographers that you need to, in town. I recognize some photographers that, work with some of the advertisements in the city".

Allison told Sara, that she was glad for the work that she had been able to complete.

Sara had not wanted to keep Allison on the phone. She wanted to give Allison an update on her design business.

Lynn had been at school.

Edgar and Allison had taken Sammy to see the dog groomer.

Joyce Eagleston had been glad to see Sammy. She told, Allison, and Lowell, that she had not seen Sammy in a while. The groomer gave her a bath.

"As long as Sammy continues to eat the correct foods, then she will continue to be strong".

Allison and Edgar left the building.

Edgar suggested that Allison, and he have lunch. There had not been anywhere near the groomer's building, where they wanted to have lunch.

Edgar suggested that Sammy remain with Jean. He thought, that way, she would be home when Lynn arrived home from school. Edgar suggested that he could drive Allison, and he into the city, after they brought Sammy to Jean.

Allison knew that Edgar wanted to spend time together. She agreed that it had been a good idea. Allison had not spent time in the city in, several, months. The last time Allison spent time in the city, was when Lynn, and Allison, last brought Sammy to see Joyce Eagleston.

Edgar and Allison arrived to the home Allison shared with Lynn, and Sammy. Edgar remained in his same outfit. Allison wore a different wardrobe piece, after she gave Sammy her lunch.

Allison brought Sammy to Jean.

Allison had been ready. She began to look forward to Edgar and her spending time together.

Edgar and Allison approached the highway. She had not wanted to be gone for more than, several, hours.

At two that afternoon, Edgar and Allison arrived to the restaurant.

Edgar decided on a restaurant that he visited in the past. It had been one of his favorite places to dine.

Edgar and Allison were seated.

The server approached them. She looked, as if, she had, a long day. The server had been pleasant with them.

Edgar began to talk about the peace organization. They had gone to many places. Edgar enjoyed assisting people that needed the assistance of the peace organization. They were able to give people better supplies and shelter. The peace organization raised more finances, and that gave them an opportunity to assist more people.

The organization was thinking of changing some of their policies.

"This is a good thing for them. I never know what to expect, until we have a meeting".

Edgar continued talking, and Allison and he finished their conversation.

After Edgar and Allison finished eating at the restaurant, Edgar brought Allison home.

Lynn had been waiting for Allison to arrive home. She had been drawing, and heard Allison walk through the door.

Jean greeted Allison.

"I was starting to become worried for you".

Allison walked toward her daughter, and had given her a hug.

Lynn asked Allison about her date with Edgar.

Allison reminded Lynn, that it was not a date.

"We are staying acquainted. Edgar did ask about you. We decided to visit a restaurant in the city".

Lynn told Allison that she had eaten her dinner.

Jean had shown Allison a finished gown.

"I need to bring the gowns to the event hall. The gowns need to be matched with the models. There will be three other designers at the event. I assume that they will also have to have their designs turned in".

Allison knew Jean had been working hard to complete the last gown. She had been nearly as busy as Allison. Jean enjoyed being kept busy. Allison liked the design. Allison liked the vibrant colors. She had given Jean a complement on the gown.

Jean planned to bring the design, along with the other designs, the following day to the individuals in charge of the fashion event.

Jean and Allison were in the middle of a cup of tea, when the phone rang. Jean had been expecting a call from a woman to know the time to meet, to deliver the gowns. She talked, for, several, minutes on the phone. Allison noticed Jean nodding her head in agreement.

When Jean finished with the conversation, she sat across the table from Allison. She had given her the details of the meeting that was going to take place that next day. Jean was to meet the staff in order to complete all the details of her part at the fashion event.

Allison had to visit with a photographer that Hansen told her about. She planned to meet with the photographer, after she took Lynn to school.

Allison mentioned to Jean that Sara was going through a similar schedule. She had an upcoming fashion event that she was to be part of.

An hour later, Allison and Lynn walked Sammy home. It was obvious that Sammy had a long day. At least she had an opportunity to spend time with Zealand. They were having a great time being around each other.

Lynn had not asked Allison anymore questions about Edgar and she.

Allison began to clean the kitchen.

Lynn had been looking forward to spending time with Edgar the next day.

That next day, had been a similar photo shoot as in the past.

There had been a woman photographer that wanted to take photos at three different locations. She knew a lot about photography.

The photographer drove for twenty minutes after the first location.

Allison asked, several, questions, about the way the photo shoot was supposed to look.

The photographer told Allison the details of the photo shoot.

The photo shoot had been going well so far.

"I need to take some photos inside".

The photographer and Allison went inside a local art exhibit.

"They do allow us to take photos inside".

The photographer wanted to primarily focus on head photos.

"I think this location would allow us to complete what we want to accomplish".

The exhibit had been quiet at the time.

The photographer approached an attendant, and explained why they were there.

Once inside, Allison and the photographer began working. They went to a popular exhibit. They visited, several, other areas, and began to finish the photo shoot.

An hour later, the photographer and Allison went for a late lunch.

Mark had not returned to the office. He realized that he had to meet with a client. Mark hoped they would be able to meet.

Sue Anne used the day as vacation. She wanted to visit with her family for a while. They planned to be in town.

Sue Anne continued to enjoy working with the firm.

Darrell announced to the office that there would be another realtor. She had been an acquaintance of his.

Things will continue to go well for the office. Allison had known that the more relators in the office, the better opportunity for people to be assisted with buying a house.

Darrell introduced the woman as Doss. She had been showing property for a number of years. Darrell had been thinking, of the topics, he wanted to discuss, at the meeting. He had been confident that the office was running well.

Allison had been talking with Lowell on the phone. He had not mentioned anything about Daniel, or his other acquaintances that were photographers.

Lowell talked about an agency that had contacted him. The magazine staff wanted him to retake a photo shoot from the previous year. He explained that it would not be easy. His business had been busy, and they would need to be patient with him. He would have to search for the previous file.

"Companies are willing to recreate a previous photo shoot. The agency found that they had not wanted the original photos, and wanted something different. I think they want to change the location of the photo shoot".

"I feel bad for complaining to you. You are doing well with work, Allison. You understand the ideas of a photo shoot. I think the agency you are working with now, does a great job at organizing the details of a photo shoot. Every so often I call my lawyer, and ask his advice. Most situations I' am able to handle myself".

Mark approached Allison's office.

Allison had been glad to see Mark. She had not held a conversation with him, since the birthday dinner for Lynn.

Mark began to tell Allison, that Gillian found a different office to work for. Things had been going great with Anne. Mark and Gillian hired someone to assist them to take care of Anne. His mother had to attend back to her life. She had a husband that she was living with. Things were beginning to stabilize for the family.

"I' am glad, that we have someone to assist us with Anne".

Mark was busy assisting, several, clients with their houses, at this time.

"I' am working with a client at this time. They are debating if they want to sell their home. They called me at the office, several, times. At some time today, we are supposed to meet. They had an appointment earlier today. After that, they are supposed to have available time. I hope that they get a hold of me. We have been talking for a while about them possibly buying another house.

Mark and Allison talked for a while.

Allison had not had work that she had to immediately complete.

Allison began to think of her current work with modeling. She was glad that she was able to talk with Lowell, because he understood modeling. Allison knew that Lowell had a lot of responsibility with his work.

In real estate, people had to have a great amount of patience. Allison understood the details of selling houses.

Mark told Allison that he began to understand real estate more, over the years. He continued to work with clients in, several, different offices. Mark had not minded selling houses.

Mark continued to talk for, several, minutes, before Allison reminded him, that she needs to sort through some future work.

Mark was waiting to finish his follow up meetings, with several clients. He was unsure how things would turn out.

Things had become quiet in the office.

Allison walked to her car. She remained concerned of the incidents that had been happening around the building. Allison hoped that Lynn was enjoying her afternoon with Edgar. He had wanted them to do some activities together.

When Allison arrived home, Sammy had been resting on the floor. She was content. Sammy opened her eyes, when she noticed Allison had come home from work. She had been glad to see Allison. Sammy had been alone all day.

Allison let Sammy wander around outside, for, several, minutes.

Sammy wanted to come inside. She drank water from her water bowl.

Allison heard the front door open, as Lynn and Edgar came inside with, several, bags. There had been, several, bags left inside the car. Edgar went outside to retrieve them.

Edgar came into the kitchen.

"I had a great time today. I did not intend for us to do as much shopping as we had. I wanted us to complete, an activity together. Lynn insisted that we buy some things. I guess she became interested in shopping. Afterwards, we decided to go to a restaurant, and have lunch".

Edgar and Lynn were glad to be home.

Edgar began drinking warmed tea. It was becoming cooler outside. It was difficult to avoid wearing a coat.

"After all the excitement, we did not complete any Christmas shopping. Maybe we can make an attempt within the next, several, days".

Allison had been glad, that Lynn and Edgar were able to complete, an activity together.

Edgar had plans the next day.

Allison thought that maybe it had to do with the peace organization.

Lynn began to describe the restaurant.

"There had been, several, people there. It had dimmed lights".

Lynn had a great time at the restaurant with Edgar. She had been a young girl that had a chance to spend time with her father.

Edgar had begun another cup of tea.

Edgar and Allison wanted Lynn to have, encouraging surroundings.

Edgar left the home, after his second cup of tea.

Edgar realized the time, and thought that he should go. He had a meeting, that next morning.

Edgar told Sammy goodbye.

She propped her head up, because she understood him.

Edgar mentioned that he enjoyed the day.

Lynn had not had anything new to share, about school. She mentioned that there had not been much happening at school.

"I know that you would not date Edgar".

Allison assisted Lynn to put things away in her closet.

Allison assisted Lynn in picking out an outfit for the next day.

Lynn wanted to remain in her room, and spend some time drawing.

Lynn told Allison, that she had seen a beautiful outdoor scene, when Edgar and she had walked that afternoon. There had been an area with benches where people were able to sit. There had been a stand that was selling different items. The sky assisted in making the scene feel familiar. Edgar and Lynn had walked through some boutiques.

Allison left Lynn alone, so she could draw.

Allison had been glad that Lynn had been thinking of her father. Edgar had been waiting to buy a house. The realtor was still finalizing the contract. Edgar decided to rent a small property, until the documents were completed. Allison felt that the peace organization had been good for Edgar. He enjoyed being able to assist other people with relief efforts.

Lynn continued drawing, as Allison made a call. She wanted to talk with Lowell. Allison wanted to talk with him about her photo shoot. Things had gone well.

Lowell had been busy that day.

Lowell explained that he had three photo shoots that day. The photo shoots had taken a while to complete.

"I had not had as hectic of a day, as today, in a while".

Allison could hear his subdued tone through the phone. She thought that maybe he had come across an issue during the photo shoot.

"I have to say, it is nice to meet different people. I have always known that being a photographer would allow me to see a lot of different personalities. After I took, several, photos, I knew that, it would be something that I would complete for a while".

"I' am glad, that Edgar and you get along well enough. I' am sure, that Lynn appreciates the time that she is spending with Edgar. If Lynn were my daughter, I would want the best for her".

"Allison, I do not want us to have to worry about our communication at this time. I enjoy your company the way we are. I would rather not analyze our relationship at this time".

Allison knew that Lowell had not known if Edgar and she would begin dating. He often expressed his concern about her raising Lynn by herself. Allison reminded Lowell, in the past that Lynn, and she were doing fine. Lynn had been a great gift to Edgar, and she.

Allison thought about the new acquaintances that she made. Things had been difficult for her at first.

Allison told Lowell, that Edgar felt the same way about their relationship.

It had been initially overwhelming for Edgar, and Allison, to go through a divorce.

"That is why Lowell, had chosen to remain in contact with Lynn".

Allison knew that Lowell had not intended to pry into her life. She thought it was best for Edgar, to be part of Lynn's growing up. Edgar understood the changes in her life, and had not pressured her, for information about the details of her life at this time.

Lowell reminded Allison, that she had been doing a great job, and, that he would talk with her soon.

Allison agreed that they had been on the phone for a while, and should talk later.

Allison began to feel her long day fade away.

Allison felt alert, by the time Lowell, and she ended their conversation. She did not want to drink another cup of coffee. It would keep her awake.

Allison had not talked with Jean in two days. She had things that kept her busy. Jean planned to attend the holiday dinner, in several, weeks.

Allison had been in the office for the earlier part of the day. She had been working on completing, several, loans. Allison had planned to get the loans completed.

The loans being completed depended on if the client wanted the contract with Delkes Realty.

Mark called Allison. He told her that he would be inside the office later.

Allison listened to Mark.

Things at this time were inconsistent for Mark. He had become used to this. Mark told Allison, that David had grown even taller since the last time that Allison and Lynn had seen him.

Allison had been glad for Mark and Gillian.

Doss had not arrived inside the office.

It was not like Doss to arrive late.

"I know that you are glad that David is healthy".

Allison and Mark talked for, several, minutes. Mark wanted to clear his phone line, in case Gillian had been trying to contact him.

The winds outside had been strong.

Allison continued with her work. Allison had not known what she would do, if Jean had not been available to keep Lynn company, during the day.

Even with Jean working on her gowns, she kept Lynn company.

Allison also knew that at this time, Edgar was not working as much as he had in the past.

Mark came inside the office, an hour later.

Mark had been in good spirits.

"At least, that was resolved".

"Gillian had mechanical issues with her car. There had been a mechanic, several, miles away. Gillian said that the mechanic had been able to fix the issue. Afterward, she had been able to go directly to the office".

"Now, I' am able to get some work done. I think Doss enjoys working at this firm. I do not think that she will leave the firm anytime soon".

Allison began thinking about Lynn.

Lynn recently told Allison, about the games the students played during their free time. Whenever a student learned a new game, they would teach it to the rest of the students. Lynn was having a great time, at her school. The students wanted to learn from each other.

Allison imagined that it had been the same way for her when she was younger. There were things that Allison had not remembered. She knew that her parents must have been patient with her.

Those things, that Allison did remember, she sometimes mentioned to Lynn.

Lynn enjoyed learning new things. It was encouraging for Allison as a parent.

Allison hoped, that her daughter would remember the things that kept her happy.

The life Lynn lives, was different, than the life Allison lived. Allison was trying to adjust being a single parent. She was glad Lynn, had a good sense of herself.

Allison continued to think back to the conversation, that she had with Lowell. He mentioned in the past, that it was not easy raising a child as a single parent.

Mark had been sitting at his desk, an hour later. He had some work to complete with, several, properties. Mark had meetings that he had to go to.

Occasionally, a client would not understand mortgage rates, when they looked to buy a house. They had not understood the investment they would receive on the house.

Allison knew that these were the things that kept Mark busy with real estate.

Sue Anne had taken another day off from work.

Allison knew that Sue Anne had been having, several, events going on within her family.

Mark had not heard his phone ringing minutes later.

After, several, seconds, Mark realized that he had not initially heard the phone.

When Mark answered his phone, he began talking with Gillian.

Allison noticed that Mark became intent in the conversation.

Allison had been glad for Mark and Gillian. They shared a lot in common.

Allison felt that Edgar and she never shared that same commonality.

At this time, Edgar was spending time with Lynn.

Things had been difficult for Edgar and Allison when they first decided to separate.

Mark and Gillian were on the phone for a while.

"It was Gillian. She wanted to let me know, that the person taking care of David during the day was going to pick him up from school. He had not been feeling well".

"The gentleman is working out for us at this time".

Allison knew Mark and Gillian were grateful at the time they were able to spend with their children.

Allison felt that Lynn being young, needed someone to keep her company.

Mark knew that Allison had been thinking about her daughter.

Mark asked Allison about Doss. He wondered why she had not come inside the office, that day.

Allison told Mark, that she had meetings that lasted throughout the day, the past, several, days.

Allison had been coming in and out the office.

Thus far, Doss had not needed Allison to complete a loan.

Mark spoke.

"I know that Doss had a real estate office of her own. She hired her own loan processor. I' am unsure of why Doss decided to close the office. It may have something to do with the organization. That is why I decided to work underneath a broker".

"I was thinking about opening up my own office at one time, but Gillian and I decided against it. I have a difficult time trying to organize the work that I have now. Gillian and I could not see ourselves spending even more time away from David. Our decision may be similar to yours".

"Part of the reason you chose not to sell houses anymore, is because the amount of time you would spend away from Lynn. If Gillian and I figure out a solution, then we may change our minds".

Mark told Allison, that he had been concerned, about Doss.

Allison had been at her desk working. There had not been much work left for her to do. The work has been slowing down for the office. Allison had prepared to leave that day.

Mark told Allison, that he planned to remain inside the office for another hour.

Allison remained cautious, as she walked out to her car. She slowly opened the car door, and stepped inside her car. Allison drove home.

Lynn had been outside with Sammy and Zealand.

Jean noticed Allison.

Jean had come outside.

"The event staff called me, and they liked the designs of the gowns. They had not mentioned anything else to me, when I brought them the gowns. They plan to give me more information".

Jean had been busy with the fashion event. Jean asked Allison about Sara.

Sara had planned to be part of a fashion event.

Allison told Jean, that she had not talked with Sara.

"Hopefully, I will be able to talk with her in the near future".

Allison was inside the office.

Allison heard her phone ringing. She thought that it may have to do with Lynn. Edgar may also be trying to contact Allison.

When Allison answered the phone, she realized it was Sara.

Allison had not talked with Sara in, several, days.

Sara told Allison similar news, as Jean had, several, days ago. She provided, several, gowns to a fashion event. It was too early, to have all the details. Sara hoped that she was able to have more people interested in her designs. She decided to keep her boutique opened for the time being.

"Allison, I have no idea what I would do, if you had not assisted me in the past with my designs. You were a great asset to my designs. I do appreciate, that you modeled some of my designs".

Sara asked Allison, about any photo shoots, that she had coming up.

Allison told Sara, that she had not been in contact with Hansen. She knew that she would have another photo shoot, within the next, several, weeks.

"Later today, I do need to place a call to Hansen".

Sara wished her luck.

"Things will go well Allison".

Allison told Sara, that she would finish up some work inside the office, and then have a meeting with a client to process a loan. Allison told Sara, that the meeting should not take long.

Allison and Sara talked for, several, moments, before Allison ended their phone conversation. Allison had not wanted to have her office phone tied up for too long. Someone may be trying to contact her.

After the conversation, Allison drove to an office. She was to meet a gentleman that was a Vice President of a firm.

The gentleman had been busy with work.

Allison took out the documents that the gentleman needed to sign. He was appreciative that they were able to conclude on the loan.

The gentleman and Allison were in the middle of the meeting inside his office. He asked her, several, questions about the contract. Allison answered the questions of the gentleman.

Several, minutes later, the gentleman and Allison walked along a path.

People around them, may have thought they were more than business associates.

Allison had not been as familiar with the part of town. She thought that it was a beautiful area. The sun was beginning to set.

The gentleman apologized to Allison for keeping her. He had set aside some time for the meeting. The gentleman had been glad that all the details had been in place for him to purchase the house. He had not known the plans that Allison may have had that day.

Allison told the gentleman that she did not mind the meeting. Things were slower for the office this time of year. Allison had not had another meeting to go to that day.

Allison had not known the personal life of the gentleman. Usually a client mentioned something to her. The gentleman was the sort of person that carried, a lot of life experience with him.

Allison noticed the salt and pepper streaks the gentleman had in his hair.

Allison and the gentleman continued to walk.

The gentleman told Allison, that it had been, the second bank, he worked for. His father had been into investments, and encouraged him to stay with the particular bank, after he left the other office. The gentleman told Allison the bank worked out for him. They made him Vice President fifteen years ago. He had not minded the position.

"I have managed to raise my children working for the bank. Early in my career, I decided that I wanted to know finance".

The gentleman told Allison that he managed to hire, several, great bankers that worked for the company for some time.

"Afterwards, some of them decided to open their own consulting firms".

"The financial business takes some people, several, years, to understand".

The gentleman told Allison, that when he first began in finance, things had been overwhelming for him. Once he received, several, clients, things became easier for him. Clients were referring other people to the gentleman. This had been working out for him. The gentleman had been unsure, if he would open a third office.

"I have business associates with backgrounds in finance that may assist me".

Allison and the gentleman continued to walk.

They found Allison's car.

The gentleman thanked Allison for her assistance, and reminded her, that he would be in contact with the office.

Allison had been glad that she had a chance to have the meeting. He had similar worries as her. He enjoyed his career.

Allison drove home. She was concerned about Sammy. Allison hoped that Lynn remembered to feed Sammy. She had been used to being taken for a walk in the late afternoons.

Allison arrived home.

Sammy walked from her water bowl, to Allison.

Sammy was glad to get attention from Allison.

Sammy became more outgoing, once she had become used to her new home.

Lynn had come from the dining room.

Lynn had been drawing.

Lynn told Allison, that there had been a student in the class that asked her about an in class assignment. She had not known him as well. He had normally been a quiet person. Lynn told Allison that she had not, wanted to get into trouble during class. The student decided to ask the teacher.

Allison told her daughter that she had not blamed her. The teacher would not have appreciated the class being distracted.

Lynn had gone to, several, events with her acquaintances from class. Lynn had not asked Allison in a while, to take her to meet her acquaintances. Allison knew that Lynn would grow out of wanting to spend, as much time at home.

Allison thought of the plans for the upcoming holiday. Jean planned to visit her family. She, and her brother, put together the plans for her to visit the family.

This time, Jean asked Allison and Lynn to take care of Zealand. He had not been feeling well the past, several, days. He developed an ear infection, several, days ago.

"I brought him to the emergency room, and he will need to take medication for several weeks. The veterinarian said that his ear infection will heal in, several, days. By the time I visit my family, everything will be fine with Zealand".

Allison thought about the last appointment that she took Sammy to. Lynn had come with her.

Allison hoped that her daughter would not become disappointed, if Edgar decided to leave with the peace organization. At this time, they had been spending time together. They continued to make plans at least twice a week. Allison had not spent as much time talking with Edgar. She had not wanted to interfere with Edgar and Lynn spending time together. Allison decided that she would keep with her schedule.

Allison remembered Lynn's most recent conversation with Edgar. Lynn continued to talk to him on updates about the class. He enjoyed their conversations. Lynn had not had any concerns other than her work in class.

Lynn continued drawing. She was enjoying practicing her talent. Lynn had become more proficient, than she had been before.

Lynn told Allison that the class had another hamster, and it had grown bigger. Ms. Rosner promised to buy them another hamster about a month ago.

Allison listened when Lynn told her this.

Lynn would feel bad if something happened to the class pet. She told Allison, that the hamster stayed inside the classroom overnight.

Sammy had come and sat next to Lynn.

While Lynn drew, Allison went next door to talk with Jean. She had been outside, with Zealand.

"Today my schedule was similar to yours. I arrived home, several, minutes ago. Zealand had not been walked all day. He is glad that he was able to come outside. I think that he can endure the cold weather better than I can. I had to put on two sweaters to remain outside. The winds today are not bad. If they had picked up, then we would not have gone outside".

Zealand had been wandering around.

Jean and Allison walked Zealand.

Jean and Allison began talking about Jean's design career. She had then, begun creating new ideas for another gown. Jean was in the process of putting together some of the detail. She wanted to create something that was different from the other designs that she created in the past. Jean had begun a design, and then changed her mind.

"I enjoy the design on the back of the gown".

Several, minutes later, Jean had decided to return inside.

Allison left for her home. She hoped that Jean would find the design that she wanted.

Lynn added food for Sammy.

Sammy finished eating.

He walked toward Lynn.

Allison prepared soup for dinner.

Allison and Lynn ate.

Allison and Lynn had not wanted to eat anything different.

Allison reminded Lynn not to feed Sammy the foods that they eat. It would not be good for her health.

Today, Allison had not planned to go inside the office. She had another photo shoot opportunity that Hansen scheduled for her. Allison had to meet the photographer, in, several, hours.

Allison found the woman.

The photographer had equipment with her. The woman recognized Allison, from photos she had seen.

The photographer walked toward Allison, and handed her a cup of coffee.

"I thought that you may need this, to awake you".

Allison took the cup of coffee.

The photographer continued to drink from her cup of coffee.

"There are, several, scenes that would be great, for this particular photo shoot. I' am sure, that you are used to photo shoots. I think today, we should be able to obtain, several, great photos".

The photographer was glad, that Allison was prepared.

The photographer began taking, several, photos.

The staff changed the scene.

The photographer took more photos.

Allison continued to work with the photographer, as they finished the photo shoot.

The photographer realized, that she had to make a phone call, because of another obligation that she had. She had not known how long it would take. The photographer had to locate an office with a phone. The photographer told Allison that she understood if she was unable to wait to finish the photo shoot. She told Allison that she would contact her at a later time.

Allison waited for a half hour.

Allison had decided to read through, several, magazines, she brought with her. Allison thought that this may create new ideas for her.

Allison noticed the photographer walking toward her.

The photographer said, that the agency asked her to take more photos of the city.

"I reminded them, that I would need to finish, several, projects first".

The photographer and Allison finished the photo shoot.

Allison and the photographer, walked to their cars together.

Allison was at home.

Lynn had been at school. She would be there for at least another three hours.

Allison decided to take Sammy for a walk. She would go inside the office afterwards.

The trees were covered in the crystalized snow that had fallen, the day before. It was beautiful, before, the holiday.

Allison thought about Christmas. She would invite Edgar to the holiday plans.

Allison arrived to the office.

Doss had been busy with work.

Doss told Allison, that she had been working on some client files. She was concerned at the time the house was taking to sell, for a recent client. Doss planned to keep working on the sell.

"Real Estate can be a long process at times. I was at the previous office for, several, years. There were, several, people that had worked, there the whole time I had been there. We managed to sell a lot of houses".

Doss told Allison that she had another meeting that she had to attend. A gentleman wanted to buy a second house. The houses were located in the city.

Doss said, that she would return that next morning.

By the time Doss goes to the meeting, and an early dinner, it will be time for the office to close. She hoped that the house would sell. Doss promised Allison, that they would talk at a later time.

That had been the longest conversation Allison had with Doss. She was straight forward. Allison enjoyed talking with the other individuals inside the office.

An hour later, Allison remained at the office. She had not had any work to complete at the time.

Lowell called Allison at her office, and told Allison, that the photo shoot he had, went well.

"The agency called me, and wanted me to do future photo shoots with them. They asked about you. They thought, that maybe, they might have some upcoming work".

Lowell continued talking. He told Allison, about the drive into the city he planned to take, to visit another photographer.

"Daniel is dating a woman that he wants to marry. He had not mentioned it to me before. We have been close acquaintances for some time. Allison, I had not wanted to attend their dinner by myself. I was wondering if you wanted to come into the city with me".

Allison had thought that it would be a nice idea.

Lowell had talked of Daniel, on, several, occasions. She would finally be able to meet him. Allison would ask Edgar, if he and Lynn planned on spending time together. If not, she would make some form of arrangements, so her daughter would not be left alone, while she was gone.

Lowell told Allison, that he was glad, that she would come to the dinner with him.

Allison told Lowell, that she would have to rearrange her schedule, if Hansen called from the agency. As for now, Allison planned to keep her current work schedule for the week.

Allison and Lowell talked about real estate.

Lowell had been thinking of selling his current home, and purchasing another. The home he had been living in had become the same to him. Lowell wanted a different studio for his photography. He mentioned that the process had taken a while, to buy his current home. Lowell planned to have more space. Therefore, he was considering a different purchase amount.

Allison and Lowell ended their conversation.

Lowell told Allison, that he would call her later. He had work that he needed to complete.

Allison had been glad, that Lowell called her. He picked a good time to want to reach her.

Allison worked inside her office a while longer. The time had been going fast.

Sue Anne or Darrell had not come inside the office. Darrell had a family situation that he had to attend to. He had not told anyone the full situation. Everyone inside the office knew that his mother had been ill. She had gone into the hospital last week.

Hansen called Allison at her office.

Hansen told Allison that her photos had arrived inside his office. She would be able to view them at any time. Allison would be able to make any recommendations, as to what photos, should specifically be used for the advertisement. If she had been unable to decide, he would choose the photos.

Allison and Hansen had continued with their brief conference. It lasted for another hour. Allison informed Hansen, that she should not take any more work for a while. She had completed, several, projects recently. Allison planned to take, several, days off from modeling.

Hansen told Allison that he understood.

"You will have more of an opportunity to spend time with your family".

It took Lowell and Allison, nearly two hours to arrive to the home of Daniel and Amy.

Daniel and Amy welcomed Lowell, and Allison.

Daniel introduced Lowell, and Allison to Amy.

Amy mentioned that she had been glad to be there. She mentioned her young son, Andrew from a previous marriage. He had not been there with them. Amy thought that it was not the right time to involve Andrew, in all the activities, Daniel, and she completed together.

Allison mentioned to Amy, that she was going through a similar situation. Her previous spouse, and daughter decided to complete an activity that day.

Amy had gone into finance. She decided to work for a bank.

"I think with my experience, it was easier for me to take this career path. I' am glad that I have become the Vice President of the bank that I work for. The bank manages a lot of accounts. Whenever, I do go out of the city for work, Andrew comes with me. He is used to traveling. He has told me that he does not mind".

An hour later, everyone began drinking coffee. They became involved in their conversation, and began to discuss their previous relationships.

It had not been easy for Daniel either. He dated a woman for, several, years. He mentioned that he eventually took some time away from dating, and felt better. Daniel then met Amy.

Daniel asked Allison about her modeling career, and the way she began.

Allison explained the length of time that Lowell and she had been working together. Allison knew that eventually, she planned to no longer work in real estate.

Daniel began to understand the busy schedule Allison had.

Daniel had not planned to change his photography career.

Daniel and Amy admired the dedication Allison had toward her career.

The home displayed a Christmas tree for the holidays. It had, several, ornaments and bulbs throughout the entire tree.

Amy noticed everyone had become focused on the tree. Daniel, Andrew, and she, decided to decorate and display it a week ago.

"Andrew and I have been spending more time here, than we do our home. We had not displayed a tree this year, even though we do have a wreath on our door. That was something that Andrew and I wanted to do. We have enjoyed this holiday season. Andrew is out of school at this time. I have to say, that we had never gone without a Christmas tree, until a year ago, when I first met Daniel".

"Daniel and I were visiting the same restaurant for close to a year. We visited to drink coffee. He approached me, and suggested that we drink a cup of coffee together. We did this, several, times during lunch. He works, several, blocks away from the restaurant. I work in the same area. We continued to make plans to spend time at the restaurant".

"We decided to date. We included Andrew in the conversations. Daniel met Andrew. He became used to being around Daniel".

"I often think about this time period".

The dinner continued to go on.

Lowell had almost finished with the cup of coffee that he had been drinking. He must have had something on his mind, because he had not said as much. He watched everyone else for, several, moments.

Lowell brought up his career. He thought that it had come a long way since when he first began. He had taken a while to learn photography. Similar to Daniel, Lowell had been taking photos for a number of years. Things had become easier for him over time. Lowell had taken a while to establish his photography career.

"I have a lot of work to do in the next, several, weeks. I' am having a great time with my career. There is not any other work I rather do".

Everyone understood how Lowell felt about his career.

Daniel mentioned that he invited Lowell and Allison to dinner, before Christmas, because he had not known their plans for the holidays.

Everyone was having a great time together.

Lowell agreed that Daniel had been correct. He had not known his exact plans for Christmas.

The dinner continued.

Amy talked of Andrew.

Amy mentioned, that she would like for Andrew to begin piano lessons. He would be able to learn the notes. Amy talked with, several, people that had been willing to teach Andrew.

Andrew expressed interest in music.

Everyone continued to listen to Amy. She had been grateful to have her son. Amy had been looking forward to her future plans with Daniel. Things continued to become better for them.

Allison noticed Daniel give Amy an encouraging smile. They must have been thinking similar thoughts.

Daniel mentioned that when Amy and he decided to become married, they would most likely sell their homes, and buy one together.

"Allison, your office could assist us with the purchase of a house. We are familiar with Delkes Realty. We know that your office would give us great recommendations. I' am unsure about your future plans with real estate".

Allison told Daniel, that the office could assist, Amy and him.

Lowell and Allison were offered another cup of coffee, before they left. Everyone remained grateful, thinking about the holidays.

Allison decided to invite Daniel, Amy, and Andrew for Christmas dinner. Allison was unsure if Lowell would come to the dinner.

Allison and Lowell left the dinner.

Lowell told Allison that he was glad, that they were able spend time with Daniel, and Amy.

"Daniel has always remained the reserved person out of all our acquaintances. Recently, we have not seen each other as often as in the past. I' am sure that Daniel and Amy will continue to do well together. He has told me, that at first, he thought it would be difficult for him to assist her with raising her child. Andrew has been pleasant toward Daniel. He does not have any contact with his father. I' am unsure of the reason. Daniel does enjoy the time that he has been spending with Andrew".

Allison mentioned to Lowell, that she agree that Daniel and Amy are happy together.

"At least, Daniel, Amy, and Andrew are having a great time together. I know they feel as if they are already a family".

Lowell thanked Allison for inviting him to her Christmas dinner.

That evening had been the first time Lowell heard about the dinner.

"I had not known that you planned on having a Christmas dinner".

Allison thought it would be nice if Lynn and she invited people to their home. It had been a while since they hosted a Christmas dinner. Allison thought that it would be a good way for Lynn and her to enjoy their holiday. She planned to buy, Lynn, several, things for the holiday. Her daughter knew that her father would be at the dinner. Lynn looked forward to spending time with Edgar.

An hour later, Lowell and Allison stopped by a nearby restaurant for coffee.

Allison arrived home.

Lynn had been sleeping in her room. Jean was reading the newspaper.

"I thought, since it was becoming late, that we would come back to your home. That way, Lynn could get some rest. She told me she will take an exam tomorrow. It is her first arithmetic exam in two weeks. Lynn told me she is nervous to take it, because she had not known how to study for it".

"Jean, I know that she will do well. Things have been moving fast for her this year. Lynn will be thinking about the following school year, soon. She has already made acquaintances in the class. Lynn has been attempting to receive her proper rest".

"We prepared dinner together. Lynn assisted me with some of my design work. She worked with me for an hour. I continued to work, while she took Sammy for a walk. I hope, that Lynn does not, catch a cold".

Jean began to put away her design materials. She had not wanted to stay long. Jean knew that Allison must have been tired, after riding in the car for, several, hours.

After an hour, Allison answered a call from Lowell.

Lowell wanted to let Allison know that he had arrived home.

Allison had been glad that Lowell thought of her. She had often done the same thing, if she were driving away from meeting someone.

Allison finished straightening the downstairs. She had not heard Lynn awake, and let her continue resting in her room. Allison was glad that in such a short time period, that she had begun to feel close to Lowell. He assisted her by being involved with her career. Allison wanted to continue to be around Lowell. Things remained quiet for her at home.

Allison arrived inside the office.

Mark had been there. He was preparing to meet a client in the late morning.

"Sometimes, I' am unable to complete all of my work at the office. Today, I have a meeting with a prospective client. I' am used to it. I do not receive all the necessary information from a prospective client, until later. There are times, that I have a conflicting schedule, when I' am trying to meet a client".

Mark had not expected a response from Allison.

Allison knew that she could expect to process, several, loans, that day.

Doss carried a stack of papers. She had not said much. Doss had been that way at the office. She was getting used to being in a new office.

"My daughter asked me, if she could go out with, several, acquaintances this weekend. I told her that it was her decision. That as long as she arrived home by her curfew, that I had not minded".

That was the only personal conversation that Doss had inside the office that day. She left the area by Allison, and went to make a phone call.

Doss was on a conference call with a prospective client. By the time they ended their phone conversation, Doss looked, as if she were concerned. The gentleman asked her a lot of questions.

"The prospective client that I had been on the phone with had been a referral. His neighbor had recently moved with our agency. I have been trying to assist him in deciding on a house. I' am sure, that the client will be disappointed if he is unable to sell his current home, as quickly, as he intended".

Allison listened to Doss.

Allison reassured Doss, that things would work out for her. She did not have anything to worry about. There would always be other people interested in buying a house.

Allison reminded Doss, that Delkes Realty had not been any different than the previous office she worked at. Sells on houses would not always go, as quickly, as initially intended.

"I' am sure that you will be calling me to process more loans for you. I would give it time".

Doss felt better by the time Allison and she, finished their conversation.

Allison had met with another client, before she picked Lynn up from school.

When Allison saw her daughter, she had been glad to end her school day. Allison knew her daughter would continue to update her, about the acquaintances she had in the class.

The next day, Allison stayed inside the office, and completed some work. She had, several, files that she wanted to look through.

There had not been any recent incidents occurring around the office. Recently, there had been more people walking through the building.

It had been early evening, and the other offices were closed. Allison had been close to locking up the office.

Sue Anne called earlier, and wanted Allison to be careful. Another person from the building, informed Allison to be cautious leaving later that evening.

Allison had been glad to end her day.

Hansen called her earlier, and asked her if she wanted to complete a photo shoot that next day in the city. It would be for an advertisement that would run in a monthly magazine.

Allison thought the photo shoot would be a great idea, and told Hansen that. Allison knew the photo shoot would go smoothly.

At her home, Jean began preparing a dessert for the holiday dinner.

"After you told me that there were more people coming than ourselves, I thought that I should bake a dessert".

It was a chocolate cake, and strawberries were added. The whole home smelled of coco. Allison felt that the dessert would turn out wonderful. Jean was having a great time.

"Usually, I do not spend this sort of time baking. I thought for the holiday that it would be nice to have a dessert. My mother would bake before a holiday. Since she had more immediate family over for the holidays, my mother spent more time baking in the kitchen. I do bake occasionally".

Jean continued to bake. She had been content.

"I was hoping that we could work on my latest gown".

Allison and Jean continued to talk about the town that Jean was from. Jean always shared new information with her that Allison had not known.

Allison and Jean drank coffee, as Jean continued to explain about the town where she grew up at.

There had been a handful of times that Jean had discussed her relationships with Allison.

"Everything will be ready for tomorrow".

Jean and Allison finished cleaning the kitchen.

Jean and Allison decided to work on the gown. It was difficult altering, but they were able to sew in, several, areas. There had been a zipper added to the back. Jean mentioned, that she had not decided what she planned to do with the gown.

"I guess it is always best to complete the gown first".

Allison listened to Jean.

"I do like the way the gown has turned out. I thought a lot of the original design that I created. I think the gown is unique".

Jean and Allison decided to have another cup of coffee.

Lynn had fallen asleep.

Things remained quiet, as Sammy, and Zealand rested beside Jean.

Jean asked Allison about her relationship with Edgar. She had known, that it was difficult for them, when they separated.

Allison told Jean, that things were initially busy for them. After, Edgar and she separated, was when he became part of the peace organization. Allison remembered Edgar, telling her weeks before.

"It had been a good decision for him. It is what he wanted to do".

Allison and Edgar thought about going their separate ways for a while. Edgar left some things behind when he left.

"I was concerned, that Lynn would be sad, that Edgar left with the peace organization. She had not understood at the time, that her dad would return".

Allison explained to Lynn, that they separated themselves from their relationship, and not from her.

Allison had not told Jean those details previously.

"I want her to remain a great person".

Jean sympathized, with going through the difficulty of raising Lynn, on her own.

"I almost became remarried, and I could at least understand that aspect".

Jean made herself another cup of coffee.

Jean left her design materials out.

Allison and Jean talked more about their careers, and the similarities. They planned to spend part of their day together, that next day.

Lynn awoke, the next morning.

It had been difficult for Lynn to sleep, that previous evening. Christmas Eve was, that way for most families.

Allison and Lynn exchanged gifts.

Allison had given Lynn the books, and necklace. Lynn enjoyed them. She planned to wear the necklace, that day.

Lynn bought a neck tie for Edgar. She knew that he would enjoy it.

Allison and Lynn ate breakfast.

Edgar had arrived to the home, several, hours later.

Lynn handed Edgar the wrapped box, with the tie.

Edgar unwrapped, the box, and thanked Lynn for the tie. He told her, he liked the tie.

Edgar enjoyed the smell of the home.

Edgar handed Lynn, several, wrapped gifts.

Things had been calm.

Allison had been glad, that Edgar had been able to come to the dinner.

Edgar talked to Lynn about school. He had not known what else to talk to her about. Lynn had been too young, to want to discuss many other things.

An hour later, there had been music coming from a record player. Allison placed it in front of the small fireplace.

Allison had been on a call, with, several, people from Delkes Realty.

Doss called to wish Allison and her family a wonderful holiday. She told her, that she had been at home with her two children. Her husband had been out of town. Later, Doss expected company.

An hour later, Allison was off the phone with Doss, and had already talked with Mark. Gillian and he planned to remain home with David and Anne. He thought about switching offices. He told Allison that it would depend on what office Gillian decided to work for.

Allison told Mark, that Gillian would decide on what she wanted to do.

Lowell arrived to the home of Allison and Lynn.

Lowell knew that Amy and Daniel would be coming with Andrew.

Lowell had additional photos that he wanted to show Allison. He had gone to a local park, and taken, several, photos. Lowell had always been interested in showing Allison the latest photos that he took. He thought somehow, that it would assist her with new ideas.

"I have not completed scenes, such as this in a while. Recently, I have been taking additional photos. I dislike when the photo shoot is over".

Allison listened to Lowell.

Allison viewed the photos.

Allison liked the way Lowell was able to capture some of the scenes in the photos.

Allison and Lowell sat near the fireplace.

Sammy had been keeping Lynn company.

Everyone had arrived to the dinner at the home of Allison and Lynn.

Everyone continued to talk at the dinner.

Lynn assisted Allison with preparing the table. Things had already been in order at the table. Everyone was having a great time together.

Towards the end of the evening, Daniel and Amy decided to leave the dinner. They had not wanted Andrew to fall asleep.

Hansen had given Allison a call to wish everyone a great holiday.

Jean told Allison, that she had been glad that she was able to attend the dinner.

Edgar remained at the dinner. He spent time talking with Lynn. He read, several, pages of one of her books with her.

Allison was glad that Edgar appreciated his daughter. He had been having a great time being around, his daughter, at the dinner.

Allison and Edgar drank coffee. Even though their relationship had changed, he had a great time at the dinner. Allison and Edgar talked about their lives. When they initially talked, things had been difficult at first.

Allison told Edgar, that since, meeting Lowell, that he had been assisting her with her modeling career.

Allison decided not to date at this time. She thought that it would be best to concentrate raising her daughter, and her new career.

Edgar understood Allison, as she talked.

Allison told Edgar, that Lowell had a lot of experience with photography. She had been glad that they shared that in common.

Edgar had agreed that modeling is great for her. Edgar had apologized for taking up her time that evening, and decided that he should drive home.

Allison knew that things would go well for Edgar, when he closes on his house. Mark had been doing a great job assisting him.

Allison was an hour behind.

Allison was to have a meeting with Hansen. They planned to go over some details of new work that he had for her.

Allison arrived to the office with Lynn.

Hansen told Allison, that a magazine wanted to use her photos. They would use her same current photos in the upcoming magazine issue. Allison had agreed to let them use the photos. She thought that it would be a great idea.

Allison told Hansen, that she would eventually stop working in the real estate office. She had been looking forward to switching her career. Allison told Hansen that she enjoyed modeling, and wanted to continue to go on more photo shoots.

Allison had gone to the real estate office.

Mark had been inside the office.

Mark told Allison that the manager had come by, when he first arrived.

"I explained to him that I would be switching offices in another month. Gillian had decided to keep her office position".

Allison told Mark, that she had planned, to not focus on real estate anymore.

Mark told Allison, that Delkes Realty appreciated the work that she had done. He knew that things changed in life.

"Modeling is a different career Allison".

Mark talked to Allison, about the time that his family spent together for the holiday.

"Things had gone somewhat easy for us. Everyone liked their gifts.

That was a good thing. I did not have to think about exchanging any of the gifts that were given. The best part to our day, was that we had a chance to spend time together. By the time, that we had dinner, I was unable to get the children to settle down. They wanted to spend more time with their gifts".

"Allison, if you want to do anything in the future with our families, let me know. The family would look forward to doing something, with Lynn and you. I feel bad, that we were unable to stay longer, when we came to visit Lynn and you, before the holiday".

Mark was recalling the short time his family, and he came to visit Allison, Lynn, and Sammy.

Allison had agreed with him. The children had not had a chance to see each other for long.

Mark asked Allison, several, questions about the property that he was trying to sell. He felt, that she knew as much about real estate, as he. Mark was hoping that Allison, and he could locate the problem. He had not been able to sell the house, as fast as he wanted.

Allison could understand why Mark had been concerned. He had no idea if the client would have a balance that they owed on their current home.

The afternoon went fast. After they finished looking through similar files, Mark and Allison hoped that the prospective buyer, would choose to buy the house that Delkes Realty, was selling.

"Allison, if there were more buyers, then it would make things easier".

Things did improve a little, when Mark received a call from the gentleman earlier that day. He talked with him for over an hour.

Allison told Mark goodbye, as she left the office.

Allison told Edgar, and Lynn, that she would meet them at a restaurant for dinner.

Allison found Edgar, and Lynn sitting at a table.

"We were waiting for you to arrive. We decided to order tea".

Allison sat down with Edgar, and Lynn.

Lynn began to explain to Allison, that Edgar, and she visited a Christmas tree, that was displayed nearby.

Lynn continued to lead the conversation, at least for the next hour. It was easy to listen to her youthfulness. Lynn enjoyed the attention from her parents.

The waiter introduced himself. He smiled as he starred at everyone in front of him. The waiter mentioned that he recognized Allison. He had seen her, in an advertisement, when he had gone into a boutique about a month ago. The waiter, asked Allison, if anyone else had recognized her.

Allison had been honest with the young gentleman.

Allison told the waiter, that she periodically received, several, stares, but that no one ever approached her.

The waiter thanked Edgar, Allison, and Lynn, for coming to the particular restaurant.

Allison mentioned she visited in the past. She had not thought it was necessary then, to mention her relation to Edgar.

Edgar, Allison, and Lynn finished eating.

Allison thanked the waiter for introducing himself.

Edgar, Allison, and Lynn decided to take a walk around the vicinity, before they drove home. They enjoyed their walk. The streets had been somewhat disserted, after the holiday.

Allison and Lynn arrived home, and Edgar left them.

Sammy had been glad to see Lynn and Allison.

Lynn agreed to feed Sammy.

Sammy had not eaten much since that morning. She had been fine.

Sammy wandered around, following Allison and Lynn.

Allison noticed based, on the information in the newspaper, that there would not be any snow scheduled to fall for the next, several, days.

Lynn had been in her own thoughts.

Allison was glad, that her daughter was happy. Lynn had no immediate concerns.

Allison phoned Sara, and told her that their holiday had gone well.

Sara had been doing well with her business. She entered another design into a fashion event. Sara will be featured as a new designer. Being part of the event, gave people more of an opportunity to notice the designs of Sara.

Sara mentioned that her son had been out of town, for, several, days. She said that she would be glad, when he arrived back into the city. A young woman and he had been visiting some acquaintances. Sara continued to work on her gown designs, while they were gone. Her son insisted that he wanted to visit, several, places, when they arrived home. Sara told Allison, that his work often kept him busy.

"I reminded him, that you were several hours, outside the city. He told me, that he planned to contact you".

"I will mail you the article on this particular event, when it is printed".

Allison was glad for Sara. She had come to see Sara, as a good acquaintance.

An hour later, they felt as if they had been talking for, several, minutes. Sara understood, when Allison mentioned, that she would not continue her real estate career.

Allison told Sara, that her next photo shoot, would advertise for another designer.

"That is great Allison"!

Sara told Allison, that she wished, she had more time for their conversation.

Sara spent time with her family, even though her son George was preoccupied with his life, at this time. She knew that her family enjoyed their time together. Sara's work made her happy. Everyday things continued to work out for her. Sara's, family, was one of her inspirations, to create new designs. Her amount of work increased, but she managed to complete it.

Allison and Sara ended their conversation.

Allison felt good, after talking with Sara. She had been glad, that she had been doing well. Allison knew that everyone had concerns.

There had been acquaintances that Allison had not talked to in a while. They were doing something, that kept them busy.

Lynn told Allison, that she thought that Allison had been on the phone with Edgar. She listened to the conversation, and realized, that it had been someone from the city.

That next morning, Lynn had off from school.

Lynn ate a bowl of cereal, and remained in the kitchen.

Allison and Lynn made oatmeal raisin cookies for New Year's Eve. This was a rare occasion, that they spent time together baking. There were rarely sweets in the home.

Edgar called to wish everyone, a Happy New Year's Eve! He told Allison, that he would come over for dinner.

Allison had not minded. Lynn and she would be glad to have company, at dinner.

Lynn had already finished eating, several, cookies, before Edgar arrived.

Lowell was called on a photo shoot, at the last minute. He would be gone for, several, days.

When he returned to town, Allison felt, that he would have a lot to tell her about the photo shoot. It will be surrounded by mountains. Allison remembered that Lowell had begun to look forward to the photo shoot. He told her that even though he completed numerous photo shoots, he enjoyed taking photos around mountainous areas.

Jean arrived to the home, by early evening.

Lowell had given Lynn a camera as a present, for the holiday. She wanted to take photos.

Allison, Jean, and Edgar were in, several, photos. Sammy enjoyed having photos taken of her. She had been happy.

Lynn enjoyed taking photos.

Allison was often reminded that Lynn had become older.

The evening had been calm.

Edgar and Lynn talked.

Edgar and Lynn had been playing a board game. It had been a game that Lynn never played before.

Edgar and Lynn had been enjoying the board game. They played for a while.

Edgar gave Lynn a necklace with a single opal stone. She smiled, and thanked him. Lynn found Allison to show her. She thought that it had been nice of her father to give her a gift. Edgar told Lynn, that it was in celebration of the New Year.

Edgar had been the last guest left, since Jean had gone home.

Shortly after Edgar left, Lynn had fallen asleep. Allison had not wanted to awake her.

That next day, Allison met with a photographer that planned to take the photos for the photo shoot.

The photographer had been patient with Allison with some of the initial photos.

There had been, several, other models that arrived to the photo shoot. They had been modeling for a while. They had busy schedules.

The gentleman at the photo shoot had not said much.

The gentleman had been dressed in formal wear. Allison wore a cream dress with embroider on the front. The designer chose this color for her. She wanted to advertise her new designs.

It had been snowing outside.

Allison noticed the snow through the windows. She could tell that it was covering the ground. Allison wished that Lynn could have been there with her, but she was at home watching the snow with Jean.

Allison thought about Sammy. It was close to the time for her to go, and visit the groomer. Sammy's hair had been growing. She had been older, when she came home with Allison and Lynn. Sammy had been doing well.

Edgar wanted Allison and him to retry their relationship.

Allison told him, that she would need to think about it. She wanted the best decision for Lynn. Allison had not wanted Lynn, to feel hurt if things ended between them. She had not known how much time that Edgar and she would be able to spend together. Allison would be working longer hours for a while. Edgar had been unsure if he would be leaving with the peace organization.

Allison remained at the photo shoot. She needed to take another set of photos.

An hour later, the photographer was ready for Allison to take more photos.

Allison had worn a suit. She was in another series of photos. It took a while longer than Allison would have thought. She had known that Jean had not minded staying with Lynn.

Lynn had not gone out that particular day with Edgar. He had another prior engagement that needed to be met that day. Edgar mentioned to Allison, that he had, several, meetings. He would not be home, until later that evening. Edgar had not wanted to disturb Lynn, while she was sleeping.

Lynn returned to school, that day.

The class had the same hamster.

Edgar and Lynn bought a toy for the class hamster. She planned to give it to Ms. Rosner. Edgar assisted her with picking it out. He also decided that he wanted to buy the hamster something. Lynn was glad, that she would be able to bring the hamster something, for when the class returned to school.

Ms. Rosner accepted the gift from Lynn. Ms. Rosner thanked Lynn for being thoughtful. Things were usual for her day at school.

Lynn waited until after the end of the day, before she asked Ms. Rosner about her new classroom that she would be in that next year.

When Allison arrived home, Lynn told Allison, that Ms. Rosner had talked with the class about their new classroom.

Allison knew that it would be a transitional process for Lynn. She offered then, that Lynn and she could drink a cup of warmed tea.

Allison told Lynn, that she had another photo shoot in the morning.

Allison and Lynn spent time talking for a while. They spoke about things that her daughter had been interested in.

Lynn told Allison, that she was having a great time talking with her.

Allison mentioned that it would be nice to live in the city.

"It would be nice to have things in closer proximity".

Allison realized that she had not heard from anyone that she knew. She had expected Lowell to call her.

Allison came into the lobby of the hotel. It was where she was supposed to meet an executive of an agency. The woman had modeled in the past. She was used to the business of modeling.

The woman explained the details of the photo shoot to Allison.

Allison appreciated the time the executive took going over the details of the photo shoot. They shook hands, and the woman left.

Allison waited for the photographer to meet her at the same location. They had agreed that it would be the best place to meet. The photographer planned to drive them to where the actual photo shoot was located. He had an assistant that had already been waiting for them to arrive for the photo shoot.

"I asked my assistant to attend this photo shoot, because I have a lot to do. After our photo shoot, I have another photo shoot to complete. The company has been following my work for some time. They asked me to assist them. We will not take long with the photo shoot. You may have other obligations today".

Allison appreciated the kindness of the photographer. That day, she had not had to go inside the office.

At the end of the photo shoot, Allison thought that everyone, including herself, had done a great job. Everything had been completed.

During the photo shoot, Allison felt that she was smiling for two hours. In actuality, it had been for, about an hour.

There had been no reason for anyone to remain behind, after the photo shoot. Before the photographer, and his assistant left, he told

Allison, that he would develop the film. The photographer and his assistant left.

The photo shoot had been completed.

Allison drove to the office of Hansen.

Hansen had not known where his agency would find a photographer, to complete a photo shoot, for an upcoming advertisement.

Allison suggested, they let Lowell, complete the photo shoot.

Allison explained that they were acquaintances.

Hansen thought that it had been a good idea. He told Allison, that he would contact him. Hansen mentioned that Lowell, and he had met in the past. He had been glad, that he was having success with his career.

Hansen offered Allison a glass of water.

The office of Hansen had been busy. He had a lot of things going on.

Allison had plans with Lowell, after the photo shoot. They planned to have dinner together. Lowell and Allison would visit a local art studio, after the dinner.

Allison and Lowell remained at the restaurant. They enjoyed their conversation.

Lowell had been a good acquaintance. Allison learned new things from Lowell. They had been busy working lately, and had not been able to spend, as much time together.

Allison asked Lowell about the photo shoot.

Lowell told Allison, the photo shoot went well. It was completed within, several, hours.

The art studio had been open to the public. Rarely, had the artist been there. He was usually working.

"Allison, I have seen a lot of art, but I think this is one of my favorite art studios".

"He used to leave the doors open for people to view his work. Since the photographer has grown even more popular, he decided to hire a secretary".

Several, seconds, after Lowell mentioned the details of the studio, there had been a woman, that approached Lowell and Allison. She reminded them, that the studio would be closing soon. The woman walked toward the front desk.

Lowell and Allison realized that the woman planned to remain up front.

They walked around the art studio. Lowell and Allison walked for, several, minutes. They lost track of the time.

Lowell suggested that Allison, and he have dinner sometime in the future.

Allison thought that was a great idea.

Lowell and Allison, continued a conversation of the studio, and then talked of their past experiences with their careers.

Allison liked the reserved kindness of Lowell. They were on opposite ends of their lives. Allison had Lynn from her previous marriage, and Lowell had never been married. She had not known if he would change that part of his life.

Allison and Lowell walked along a narrow street. It was busy with people trying to stay warm in the cold weather. The store fronts, had taken down their holiday signs.

The people around, may have thought, Allison and Lowell were acquaintances for a while.

Allison was at home with Lynn, and Sammy.

Lynn had not done much, that day.

Sammy began wandering around the home, as if she wanted to go for a walk.

Lynn ruffled Sammy.

Jean came to visit Allison, Lynn, and Sammy.

Jean showed Allison a pattern from a gown that she was completing. It was black. The gown would have, flower embroidery, with a chiffon bow.

Allison admired the idea of the gown. She told Jean, that she had been doing a great job. Allison thought the gown displayed a lot of creativity. Jean had not known who she would sell the gown to.

Things became quiet around the home.

Allison noticed that Lynn had fallen asleep, after keeping Sammy entertained.

Lowell invited Allison and Lynn to his home. He wanted to discuss some photos with Allison. Lowell had not minded that Allison and Lynn bring Sammy. Lynn would have company, that Saturday morning.

Allison and Lowell finished looking through some photos.

Allison and Lowell drank coffee.

Lowell heard a faint barking noise outside. He realized that it had been Sammy. He was near the edge of the marina barking.

Lowell and Allison had not seen Lynn. She had been coming in and out of the home for the past, several, hours. Lynn explained that it had been the warmest day, all season.

Lowell began calling Lynn through the noise of the water crashing against the rocks.

The worry that Lowell, and Allison began to experience, had brought on a deafening noise.

"I think that Lynn is in the water".

Lowell thought of where Lynn may be. He quickly took off his shoes, and went into the water.

Allison followed behind Lowell. She could see her daughter's hand. Allison hoped that everything would be alright. Lynn was young. Lynn had not formerly learned to swim.

Lowell carried Lynn away from the lake.

"I think that Lynn is fine".

Outside felt, to be, twenty degrees colder, to Allison. She had been worried that things would turn out bad.

After Allison called the emergency personnel, she remained with Lowell, and Lynn.

Lowell tried to revive Lynn. He noticed that she had not been immediately breathing.

Allison heard her daughter cough.

Lynn spat out water. She breathed heavily, as Lowell and Allison watched her. Lynn waited a moment, before she turned to Allison.

Allison heard Lynn call her name.

The emergency personnel walked toward the marina. The personnel offered to put Lynn on a stretcher, and bring her to the hospital. She softly told them, that she had been fine. Instead, the personnel assisted Lynn up. She stood, and looked to be fine.

"You did a great job reviving her".

Lowell and Allison walked Lynn inside his home. She rested in an adjoining room.

Allison and Lowell remained quiet, as they read through the newspaper. Sammy was solemn.

Lynn reemerged after two hours. She wanted some warmed tea. Lynn apologized to Allison for scaring her.

Sammy had awoken, and walked toward Lynn.

Lynn ruffled Sammy for, several, moments. She told Allison, that they could go home. Lynn thanked Lowell for assisting her.

On the way home, Lynn told Allison that she had been cold, and scared when she was in the lake.

When Allison and Lynn arrived home, Lynn drank another cup of warmed tea. She told Allison that she felt better, before she went to bed.

The next morning, Lynn awoke, and told Allison that she had a headache.

Allison drove Lynn to the hospital, and they visited with a doctor.

The doctor told Lynn that she would be fine, and that she had been experiencing shock, from the events of the day before.

Lynn told Allison, that she felt better.

Allison and Lynn went to visit Lowell. Sammy remained at home.

Lowell was glad, that Lynn was feeling better.

Lowell and Allison watched Lynn for, several, moments, before they looked at photos.

Lowell paused, before he mentioned to Allison that he thought they should date.

Allison thought for a moment, and told Lowell, she agreed.

Lowell kissed Allison on the lips.

Lowell and Allison spent the next, several, minutes, talking about the time, that they were spending together. They both would remember this time.

Allison was glad, that Lowell wanted to spend time together. Allison had not dated anyone, since Edgar. She had been spending a lot of time with her daughter. Lynn would continue to adjust to the changes in her life.

Allison and Lowell had plenty to talk about. She was glad, that she had the opportunity to model. Allison had a lot of stressful times with real estate. She awoke Lynn, and she drove them home.

The next morning, Allison awoke early.

Allison prepared breakfast for Lynn, and her.

Allison and Lynn sat on the patio, and ate warmed cereal. She thought that it would be a good time to tell her daughter, that she had begun dating Lowell.

Lynn thought it was a good idea, that Allison was dating Lowell.

"I think that it is a good idea".

Lynn had not expected her mother to live her life alone. Lynn knew that it was Edgar that chose a different life.

Allison had been reminded that her daughter was capable of understanding these things. She had not wanted her daughter to become concerned. Allison wanted to make sure, that she would always be part of Lynn's life.

Allison arrived at Delkes Realty.

Allison thought of the family of Mark, and he. He had not come inside the office. Allison wanted to tell Mark about the things that had been going on in her life, the past, several, days. She wanted to tell him, about the near drowning accident, that her daughter had. The accident worried Allison. She wanted to tell Mark, that Lowell, and she began dating. Lowell would spend more time, with Lynn.

Allison was at home, and decided to walk Sammy. They were gone for a half hour. Allison had been ready to bring Sammy inside. Soon, she would take her for a walk on the beach.

Allison was glad to be able to speak with Lowell. He thought they should spend time together.

Allison told Lowell, that she should stay home with Lynn. She may need assistance with an assignment from class. Lynn continued to learn new things in school.

Lowell told Allison that he understood. He knew that he would talk with her soon. He wished her luck on her photo shoot the next day.

Allison planned to retake some photos for the agency that Hansen worked for. They decided on additional photos. Allison had not minded. She had not had any other work that needed to be completed.

Lynn talked of her day in school.

Allison listened intently as her daughter talked.

When Allison arrived to meet Hansen, he had been ending a call.

"A lot of people seem to be in demand of this agency, at this time. At times, I' am busy traveling".

In the past, Hansen had completed some work as a fashion photographer. He had been gone for, several, weeks, at one time. There had been a fashion event that lasted for a while. Hansen told Allison, that he had not minded the particular photo shoot.

"I will most likely take photos, at this type of event, in the future. I enjoy traveling to complete photo shoots. I' am sure that Lowell feels the same way. Lowell and I have talked about some of the photography he has done".

Hansen had been putting some details together for an upcoming trip. He would not see any clients, until he returned. Hansen thought to ask Allison about Lowell.

Allison told Hansen, that Lowell was fine. As a photographer he enjoyed taking photos. Lowell was constantly working.

"I can imagine. I constantly have meetings. That is part of the career that I have chosen".

When Allison arrived home, Jean walked toward her, and said that something happened to Mark. He was at the hospital.

Allison had been concerned for Gillian, and their children. She realized that she needed to call their home. Allison knew the area around the office had been unsafe.

When Allison called the home of Mark, Gillian explained that Mark suffered a mild stroke, and was in the Intensive Care Unit.

"Everything is going well at this time. I know that we are acquaintances, and I wanted to call, and tell you. David and Anne are fine".

Gillian told Allison, that Mark would improve.

"Mark had been concerned about two real estate contracts. He had, several, scheduled meetings. He will have to wait a while to return to work".

Allison felt bad, that the event has happened to their family. There seemed to be constant change with life.

Lynn was watching Sammy. They were doing fine outside. Lynn told Allison, that she had not had any assignment that was due.

Allison continued to talk with Gillian.

Allison planned to visit Mark. The hospital was, several, miles away.

Gillian apologized for being in a hurry, but Mark and she needed to talk with the doctor. Mark had been stable the past, several, hours.

Allison told Gillian, that she understood. She would talk with them soon.

Allison told Jean of the situation. Jean felt bad. She thought, the situation sounded stressful.

Jean had been glad, that Allison had been doing well as a model. She knew, she herself, had been doing a lot of work on designing gowns.

Lowell was walking toward them. He asked Jean and Allison, how they had been doing. Lowell told Allison, that he knew, that she had been busy. He told her, that his day had been productive.

"I managed to organize, several, contracts. I may have possible work".

While Jean had been near, Lowell asked Allison, about the worried expression, on her face.

Allison explained that Mark had been in the hospital, due to a mild stroke. She told Lowell, that he had been stable.

Lowell asked Allison, if she wanted to visit the hospital. He offered to come with her.

Allison told him, that they could go, that next morning, to the hospital.

Allison thought that it would be best, that Lowell spent time completing some work.

Lynn noticed Lowell, and walked toward him.

Lynn gave Lowell a hug.

Jean remained with Zealand, and Sammy.

"Sammy had not gone for a walk yet".

Lynn turned toward Allison, and asked her if she could take Sammy, for a walk.

Lynn said goodbye, to Jean.

Allison told Lynn, that Lowell, and she would come with her.

The air had been crisp, as Lowell, Allison, and Lynn walked down the long street with Sammy. Lynn was content. She had been able to walk Sammy.

Lowell, Allison, and Lynn, arrived home with Sammy.

No one had eaten dinner.

Lynn wanted to assist Lowell, and Allison to prepare dinner.

They ate, at the dining room table. All three of them, had a great time. Sammy had been sitting nearby. It felt to be a normal routine for them, as if they had been eating dinner together, every night.

Lowell had not asked Lynn questions about school.

Allison had known that he was busy, with his work.

Lowell told Allison, that he had, several, things to do, that next day, but, that he wanted to visit the hospital with her.

Allison then, had been reminded of Mark.

Allison was glad, that everything had been fine with Mark. He would have to take some time off from work.

Lowell showed Allison, several, photos that he had recently taken.

Lowell promised to return, that next morning. He left the home.

Allison had taken her daughter to school, about an hour ago. She drank a warmed cup of tea, while she waited for Lowell.

Allison could hear a car outside, and had known, that it was Lowell. She met him at his car, and he drove them toward the hospital.

Allison and Lowell went inside the hospital building. She noticed Gillian. The woman looked slightly exhausted.

Gillian walked toward Allison, and Lowell. She told Allison, that her parents had ridden the train into town, and they are, at home with the children. Gillian wanted the children to receive their rest.

Allison and Lowell waited outside, the Intensive Care Unit with Gillian. They had not visited Mark, inside the room.

Gillian said the personnel, would move him, to another room.

Allison and Lowell planned to wait until Mark was moved to another room, to visit him.

Allison asked Gillian, if anyone else from the office, had come to visit.

Gillian told her, that Mary had come by yesterday. Afterward, she said, that she needed to return to work.

Allison told Gillian, that there are people at the office thinking about Mark.

Allison thought Mark, looked as if he were ready to go home. He looked rested. Mark had not said much. Allison and Lowell left the hospital.

When Lowell brought Allison home, he told her, that he would call her later.

When Allison opened the door, Sammy walked toward her.

Allison knew that meant Sammy wanted to be taken for a walk.

Allison walked Sammy for thirty minutes. She had become hesitant. Allison knew, that was a sign, that Sammy had been restless.

When Allison and Sammy arrived home, Allison added food to Sammy's bowl. Sammy was content, and had not wanted anything else.

Lynn arrived home.

"Our class hamster is growing. Ms. Rosner measured him. The class learned that it had an additional two inches in length".

Lynn paused. She almost forgot to ask Allison about Mark.

"I forgot that you visited the hospital today".

Allison had not realized that she did not update Lynn on her visit to the hospital. She told her, that Mark was doing better.

Lynn was glad, that Mark had been improving.

Lynn stopped throwing a ball for Sammy to chase. She had begun to complete her school assignment.

Allison assisted Lynn to complete her assignment for class.

Lynn began to understand the class assignment.

After Lynn finished the assignment, she thanked Allison for her assistance.

Allison and Lynn heard a knock at the door.

Allison answered the door.

Lowell had been at the door.

Lowell wanted to visit Allison and Lynn. He apologized, for his unexpected visit.

Allison had Lynn to keep her day busy, and had lost track of time. She had not realized that she had not talked with Lowell all day.

Lowell had been interested in playing a board game. They chose one, and played the game for a while. The evening was calm.

The evening went by quicker, by the time Lowell and Allison each drank a cup of coffee. Lynn finished her juice.

Lowell followed Allison into the kitchen.

"I will talk with you tomorrow".

Allison had been glad, that Lowell was around Lynn and herself. Things would become better between them, as they share new experiences together.

Allison met Hansen, the next day. She had taken Lynn to school. Hansen told her, about the photo shoot he completed. The trip went well.

"I was able to complete the photos that I needed. The photo shoot, took longer, than I thought it would".

Hansen managed to find, several, messages. He mentioned that there would be a photo shoot in two days. The photo shoot was for a designer. They needed several models for their new advertisement. The photo shoot, would last for a day.

Allison agreed to be part of the photo shoot. She thought she would enjoy completing it.

Hansen and Allison talked about her career. She enjoyed, when she had an opportunity, to talk about ideas. Hansen and Allison had become close colleagues over the past, several, months. She had been glad with her career.

Hansen looked through some files.

"I' am unsure Allison, if I will go out of town, anytime soon. It would be nice. I have meetings here".

Hansen had several calls to make, and then Allison and he, would walk out the building together.

Allison waited for Hansen to complete his work. After speaking with, several, people on the phone, he had finished his work.

As promised, Hansen walked Allison out to her car. He closed her door, once she had gotten inside.

Allison waved to Hansen, as she drove, out of the parking space. She saw him walking toward his car. Allison appreciated the kindness that Hansen had. He gave her updated information, on current photo shoots.

Allison decided to drive along the streets. There had been plenty of trees lining the sides of the roads. Allison had not taken such a drive, in a while. She was able to go through some parts of town, she had not seen before.

There had been the familiar scene of Lynn playing Frisbee with Sammy and Zealand. They were having a great time.

Allison wondered if Lynn or Sammy would notice her parking in the drive.

Sammy noticed Allison.

Sammy began walking toward Allison.

Allison waved to Jean, and her daughter. Allison had worn different clothes, and asked Lynn if she wanted to visit Mark in the hospital. He would remain in the hospital for two days.

Lynn agreed to go to the hospital with Allison. She thought it would be nice to visit her mother's colleague.

When Allison and Lynn arrived to the hospital, the personnel had been busy with their tasks.

Allison and Lynn went into the room of Mark. Children had been allowed in the area. Allison and Lynn would visit for, several, minutes. They found Mark sitting up. He had been reading a newspaper. He sat it down, and looked over at Allison and Lynn.

"My family left moments ago".

Lynn went to ask the personnel for a glass of water.

"I never realized that Lynn looked as similar as you. I' am unsure of what your previous spouse looks like. I know that sustaining the marriage had become difficult overtime".

Allison asked Mark about his family.

Mark told Allison, that there had not been any changes with Gillian's work. Gillian had been content, at the office she had been working at. He told Allison that the children had been doing well.

"Gillian thought it was the best decision to remain at her office".

"I will need to stay gone from the office, for the next, several, weeks. The past, several, days have gone by slowly. I would rather be working".

Allison knew that Mark would have to be careful for a while. Until recently, Mark had seen Lynn, when she had been a toddler.

Allison and Lynn arrived home.

Allison enjoyed that she was close with Lynn. They talked.

Sammy sat in the living room next to the sofa. She enjoyed this area.

Allison had lunch with Lowell, the next day. She had been looking forward to spending time with him. They had not talked in a day.

Lowell told Allison, that he had completed some work. He told her, that he had not been able to complete it all. The work would not be completed, until the people involved, organized, the rest of the details.

Allison reminded Lowell, that their lives were busy. She enjoyed his caring nature. Allison knew, that a lot of people involved with photography, relied on Lowell. She wondered if he would talk, about his latest photo shoot.

Lowell mentioned Daniel called him, and wanted to ask Amy to marry him.

"He knows we have been dating. He reminded me, that they had been dating a while".

Lowell brought Allison home.

When Allison arrived home, Lynn had been asleep. Jean went home. Zealand had been at home, by himself for a while.

Allison had not thought that she would meet someone similar to Lowell. She had not thought, that she would be thinking about a new life, with someone at this time.

The next day, Allison had a photo shoot, with Hansen.

Before Allison, left home, she answered the ringing phone.

Lowell was on the other end.

Lowell told Allison, that Daniel, and Amy, planned, to become married.

"Daniel, asked Amy, to marry him. Things worked out for them. I' am happy for Daniel, and Amy. They have been dating, for a while. Amy had gone, through many changes in her life, after her previous relationship. I know that, they will have a wonderful celebration. I hope you plan to attend the wedding with me. I think it would be great. Besides, I think, that Daniel, and Amy would want you there".

Allison told Lowell, that she planned to attend the wedding.

Allison reminded Lowell, that she was part of a photo shoot, that day.

"You complete a lot of photo shoots".

Allison knew that Lowell had been correct. This would be another advertisement that she will complete. Allison glanced, at a previous advertisement that she had done. She had, been grateful, for the opportunity to model. Allison felt, that she had met some nice people.

Hansen had been waiting for Allison. He could sense, that she had been thinking about something, other than the photo shoot.

Allison told Hansen, about some of the recent things that happened in her life.

The photo shoot kept Hansen, and Allison busy.

Allison decided to make a phone call to Lynn, on the phone inside the room. She reminded her, that she would be home shortly.

Hansen told Allison, as she finished her conversation, that the photo shoot had been completed.

"I had been able to get the photos that I needed".

Hansen and Allison walked to her car.

Hansen told Allison, that he was glad, that the photo shoot went well.

Allison thanked Hansen.

Hansen was rarely concerned, about a photo shoot he completed.

Lynn was home with Jean.

"Lynn is talking with Edgar".

Allison talked with Jean.

"Lynn has been keeping me busy. I have been unable to work on my design, while I' am here. At home, my designs have been keeping me preoccupied".

Jean told Allison, that she had not minded.

Lynn had not ended her conversation with Edgar. Sammy and Zealand were resting near the dining room table.

Allison realized that Lynn must have kept them busy throughout the day.

Allison smiled at Sammy and Zealand.

Lynn ended her conversation with Edgar. She wanted to invite him for dinner.

Lynn recalled the conversation to Allison.

Edgar told Lynn, that he was unsure if he would be able to make it to the dinner, this time.

Lynn accepted the response of Edgar.

Lynn began to tell Allison more of the things they talked about.

Allison listened to her daughter.

Lynn had not noticed, when Allison, initially had come home.

Within an hour, Allison, Jean, and Lynn sat down to eat dinner. The dinner went by quickly for them.

Lynn talked about the class.

After Jean and Zealand left, Lynn drew.

Allison called Gillian. She hoped that it had not been too late, and that Gillian was not putting the children to bed.

Gillian answered the phone. She had not been busy.

Allison asked Gillian about Mark. She had known that he had come home from the hospital.

"Mark is doing better. He will need less responsibility, for a while. He will improve".

After, several, minutes, Gillian gave the phone to Mark.

Mark agreed, with what, Gillian told Allison.

"I plan to return to the office, in several, weeks. I have to get approval, from my doctor".

Mark mentioned to Allison, that Sue Anne, and Darrell called him.

Mark told Allison, the things, that David had been involved in. He had, several, events going on at school.

Allison had not wanted to keep Mark on the phone.

The winds had been blowing strongly. It was evident, that there will be rain.

Allison heard loud thumping, as if someone had been knocking on her door.

Mark commented on the winds outside. He assured Allison, that everything would be fine by the next morning.

Mark told Allison, that Gillian had begun to get the children prepared for bed.

"I have to visit the doctor. It has been two weeks, since my mild stroke. The doctor wants to make sure, that I will not have, any complications".

Allison was glad, that Mark was doing well. They ended their conversation.

Mark and Allison wanted to raise their children, in similar ways.

Lynn ruffled Sammy.

Lynn assisted Allison in giving Sammy a bath. Sammy had been reluctant at first. She remained patient, and they finished giving her a bath.

Allison and Lynn assisted, Sammy dry.

"I' am glad, that you were able to meet me. I need you to choose, the photos for the advertisement".

Allison thought about the photo shoot, that Hansen and she completed. It took her, several, moments, to look through the photos.

In one of the photos, Allison selected, she wore a pant suit, by the designer.

Hansen had not needed anything else, from Allison.

Allison decided to stay a while. At dusk, Allison left the meeting, with Hansen.

"Allison, I' am unsure how you manage to get as much work done as you do".

Allison appreciated this coming from Lowell. He called, that evening. Allison enjoyed hearing Lowell's voice. He told her, that he wished, he could be at the home, with her. Lowell had been working earlier, that day.

Allison told Lowell, that it would be nice, if he were at the home, with her.

Allison and Lowell tried as best they could, to keep the communication, between them.

Lowell had not wanted to always interfere with the time, Allison spent with Lynn.

Lowell knew that Lynn enjoyed spending time with Edgar. Allison and Edgar continued to keep communication between them, because of Lynn. Allison wanted their relationship to remain that way, as Lynn became older.

Allison and Lowell made plans, to meet at a restaurant for dinner, that next day. It had been, several, days, since they gone out together.

"Allison, if you could choose another activity to do during the day, what would it be"?

Allison answered, that she would spend more time, designing gowns.

It had always been something she wanted to complete more of.

The next morning, Allison had not been feeling well.

Allison talked with Jean.

Jean agreed to take Lynn to school.

When Allison awoke, the house had been quiet.

Jean decided to stay at home, and complete some work.

Sammy had been lying next to Allison.

Allison took Sammy for a walk.

When Allison and Sammy arrived home, Sammy drank from her water bowl.

Sammy watched Allison, as she drank a cup of coffee. Things had continued to remain quiet.

Allison answered the phone.

Allison talked with Sara. She had not talked to Sara in, several, days. They talked about the design, in her latest collection of gowns.

Sara told Allison, she was thinking of adding another person at her gown boutique to assist her.

"I put a notice in the newspaper. I will find someone to assist me. It would make things easier for me. I have waited a while, to have more people creating my designs with me".

Allison and Sara ended their conversation.

Allison almost forgot that she awoke, and had not been feeling well.

Lynn came home from school.

Lynn gave Allison the updated details of the class.

Lynn told Allison, that Ms. Rosner plans to keep the class hamster, even after her current class leaves.

Lynn mentioned to Allison, that she was looking forward to the next school year.

"Some of my acquaintances are transferring to another school".

Allison told Lynn, that she was glad for her. She reminded her daughter that there were new things that she needed to learn.

Lynn agreed with Allison.

Allison and Lynn focused their drawings on animals. Allison drew an elephant, while Lynn drew a horse. When they finished, they sat their drawings aside.

Allison told Lynn, that if she wanted to study art in the future, that she could.

Allison suggested that Lowell assist them with preparing dinner.

Allison dialed the telephone number to invite Lowell to dinner.

Lowell decided that he would come to their home.

"That is nice, that Lynn and you have invited me to dinner. It is nice, when I' am able to visit Lynn and you".

Allison agreed that Lynn and she were glad that he was coming to dinner.

Allison continued to talk with Lowell for a while. They ended their conversation.

Allison told Lowell, that Lynn and she would wait for him to arrive.

Allison was looking forward to seeing Lowell. He appreciated her daughter and herself.

Allison let Lowell inside when he arrived. Lynn was shy. Lynn had not spent the past, several, days with Lowell.

Lowell, Allison, and Lynn did their part toward the dinner. Lynn enjoyed making a simple bread loaf.

Lynn showed Lowell her latest drawings. He told her, that he liked them.

Lowell had an early day scheduled that next day.

"I have to develop film from a photo shoot I completed two days ago. It takes a while, before things can come together".

Allison was glad for Lowell. He had always done a great job with photography.

Lowell looked, as if he had, a long day.

Allison knew that their schedules would not always, be as hectic.

Lowell continued to finish his cup of coffee. He then said, goodbye.

Allison walked Lowell to his car.

Allison returned inside the home.

Lynn had already begun clearing the dishes. She had not minded the work.

Allison finished assisting, Lynn with the dishes.

Allison awoke. It had been raining outside.

Allison had not expected the call from Sara.

Sara told Allison about a recent client that purchased one of her gowns.

Allison wondered if she should mention that Daniel and Amy were planning their wedding.

Allison paused, before she told Sara about the wedding.

Allison gave Sara the phone number to contact Daniel and Amy.

Sara told Allison, she may be able to have Daniel and Amy as clients. They finished their conversation.

Allison and Lynn left out the door.

Lynn was at school.

Allison decided to call Mark and Gillian, when she arrived home.

Gillian answered the phone.

Gillian mentioned that Mark had been intending to call Allison. He had been busy with, several, appointments. He had been able to return to work.

Allison enjoyed talking with Gillian. They talked briefly.

Allison called Mark at his office.

He answered his phone.

Mark had been waiting to hear back from a client. He told her that even though he had been gone for a month, it felt longer.

"I had some work that required my attention. I do appreciate everyone at the office. They have assisted me to organize my work".

Allison and Mark talked about real estate for over an hour.

Mark had a call on another phone.

Mark told Allison, that he would need to talk with her some other time. He had been feeling better, since returning to work.

Allison had known that Lynn would come home soon. She would want to share the details of her day.

When Lynn arrived home, Allison and she held a conversation, about the class hamster.

Hansen was focused on his work.

"I' am trying to organize the details of this particular photo shoot. It is supposed to be completed outside. There are, several, different ideas that could be used. I will know the completed details in, several, days. I do admire some of the ideas so far".

Modeling has become a part of Allison's life. Allison is grateful at the people that took time to assist her to understand her career as a model.

Allison told Lowell, that she knew the photo shoot would go well. She liked the ideas that would be used in the photo shoot.

Hansen appreciated the compliment of Allison. He told her, that he was going to take a break for, several, minutes. Hansen asked Allison to join him.

"I' am going to visit the restaurant nearby".

Allison decided to go to the restaurant with Hansen. They left the building.

Allison had a break from her work.

The restaurant had been crowded. Allison and Hansen sat down.

Hansen asked Allison about her life.

Allison began to answer the question of Hansen.

"I have plenty of work. Photography keeps me busy".

Allison told Hansen, that she was supposed to attend a wedding soon.

"A photographer that I' am familiar with, will be having a wedding. I have not decided if Lynn will attend with me. She would like to attend".

"I am glad that you have been able to take a break".

"I agree that I have been able to spend more time with Lynn".

"I have to see what work is available. Then, I will give you the details of the photo shoot".

"I know that there is work that I would, want to be part of".

Allison appreciated the patience Hansen had toward photography. In such a short time, she managed to do a lot with her career. Allison had become busier, than she thought she would be. She told this to Hansen. Allison and Hansen had been gone for a while.

Hansen looked at his watch.

"I should go now, because I have to meet someone inside my office".

Hansen and Allison walked outside. She thanked him for the meeting.

Allison watched, as Hansen walked away. She had been ready to go home. Allison knew Lynn was waiting on her.

Allison thought, about Lowell and herself. She was glad that they had begun dating. Allison was glad, that Lynn liked being around Lowell.

Jean began walking toward Allison.

"Lynn and I completed, several, activities together".

Jean reminded Allison, that she had a great time keeping Lynn company. It gave her a break, most days from her work. Jean had not worked for anyone for, several, years.

Allison needed to complete some work in her outside garden. Allison noticed this, as she talked with Jean.

Allison managed to nearly finish working on her landscaping, when Lowell had come by to visit. He wanted to remind her of the wedding, the following afternoon.

"Allison I had not wanted you to forget. Daniel and Amy are expecting me to attend. I' am one of his closest acquaintances. I asked Daniel about Sara. Daniel and Amy had not had a chance to finalize details with her".

"It was late notice. They had the details of their wedding planned. Daniel and Amy sent Sara a card. They thank her for thinking about them".

"Amy invited Sara to the wedding. She told Amy, she was unable to attend the wedding. She had a prior engagement".

"We will enjoy ourselves at the wedding".

"Thus far, everything was going well, with the plans, for the wedding. I' am glad, for Daniel. He has been spending a lot of time, with Amy, and Andrew. Her son has been patient. Things will go well, for them".

Allison asked Jean, to keep Lynn company, when Lowell, and she, attend the wedding.

As promised, Lowell picked Allison up, midafternoon. She decided to wear a cream dress, a cream scarf, and hat.

Lowell drove them to the outside garden, where the wedding was held. Allison could see the group of individuals waiting. The afternoon went, by quickly.

They arrived to another site. It included an outdoor tent. The site was as nice, as the wedding ceremony site.

Lowell and Allison danced.

Lowell had begun to talk with, several, people that he knew. He introduced Allison to others. When it became later, they decided to leave. There had been people that had not left.

Lowell had not said much, on the way home. He knew Allison, had a long day.

Allison arrived home.

Lynn was sleeping.

Jean had been working on a new gown design. She had been glad to see Allison.

"I knew that you would not stay too long, at the wedding. I' am almost finished with another outline. I have been able to complete some work on the design".

"You are kind Jean. I know that you have a lot to keep you busy, at this time. I' am glad, that I have you here".

Allison awoke early.

Allison called Mark, to get an idea of how he was doing.

Mark answered the phone.

Mark told Allison, that he had been glad to hear from her. Things had been going well with his real estate career. Mark had a complicated contract that worked out. He had planned for another contract to go well.

"My work is improving, since I have returned to the office".

They talked about work often in the past. Mark communicated well with people. They had a lot to talk about this time.

"Some things have changed in your life. You have become divorced. I think Lowell is a good person for you to be around. He has kept Lynn and you busy. Your career has also kept you busy".

Allison talked with Mark for a while.

Mark told Allison, that she called him at a good time.

Allison mentioned that, because of her schedule that she had not been able to talk with many people other than Lowell. He and she were in similar careers.

Allison waited to see if Mark wanted to say anything else.

Allison reminded Mark, that she would stay in touch with him, and his family. She asked him to tell everyone at the office, that she had been doing well, and wished them the same.

Mark told Allison that he would.

Their children were becoming older.

Later, Allison had a chance to complete more work in her garden. Sammy sat next to her.

Sammy jumped up, and Allison knew Lynn was back at home.

Lynn ruffled their dog. Sammy enjoyed the attention.

Lynn told Allison, that she had a long day at school.

Allison nodded her head in agreement. She could understand. Allison continued working.

Allison prepared dinner, as Lynn completed her assignment for class. It had not taken her long.

Lowell joined Allison and Lynn. They ate dinner.

Sammy began eating from her food dish.

"I had nearly finished my work when Allison called me. I decided to develop some film. Normally, I' am working. I' am glad for the break".

Lowell told Allison that she would be able to see the photos, if she wanted.

Everyone was part of the conversations. The conversations remained on things that would interest Lynn. They ate the rest of the dinner.

Sammy walked toward Lynn.

Lynn gave Sammy attention. Sammy was playful.

Lowell and Allison finished cleaning.

Allison knew how to develop film, because of Lowell. They drank a cup of coffee.

The time had become late.

Lowell reminded Lynn and Allison that he had to return home. Even though he planned to take the next, several, days off, he had, several, things to do, including making calls. Lowell wanted to call Daniel, to see that his family and he continued to do well.

"He has always been more reserved. Usually I' am the one that calls him".

Allison had not expected a call, from Lowell. He wanted to tell her that he had a great time at dinner the night before.

"I wanted to talk with you".

Lowell asked Allison, if she had any plans, that day.

Allison told Lowell, that she had not, had any plans.

Lowell suggested, that Allison, and he go for a walk.

"I think it will be nice, to take a walk".

Lowell met Allison at home.

Allison watched Jean, and Lynn, watch Sammy, and Zealand, wander around outside.

Allison told Jean, that she would be taking a walk, with Lowell.

Jean told Allison, that it was fine. She would watch Lynn, and Sammy.

Lowell and Allison remained quiet for, several, moments. They had not had anything to say at that exact time, as they walked down the path to the entrance. Allison had been glad, that Lowell, and she could enjoy the calmness. Lowell wanted to ask Allison, about Edgar.

Allison knew that Lowell would want to ask her, about Edgar.

Allison mentioned Edgar.

Lowell glanced at Allison.

"Allison, I was wondering about Edgar. I do not intend to intrude in your life".

"Edgar and I agreed that it would be best, that we divorced. He is involved with the peace organization. As you know, he does spend time, with Lynn".

Lowell thought that it was a good idea, that Edgar and Lynn remain close.

Lowell and Allison began walking toward home.

Lynn waved at them. She was glad to see them.

Lynn asked Lowell, if he had planned to stay for dinner.

Lowell responded that he would.

Allison then invited Jean to dinner.

Jean told Allison earlier, that she had not any other plans that day.

The time went by fast. Everyone was eating.

Sammy and Zealand remained quiet, and patient.

Lynn joined in the conversation at the table.

Everyone realized, they had been together for a while that evening.

Jean mentioned a new design that she had been working on. She planned to sell it to a boutique that was in the area.

Jean had been the first to leave. She had some things to do that next day.

Jean smiled, as Lynn waved to her, as she left.

Later, Lynn had fallen asleep.

Lowell told Allison, that he would see her, that next day.

Allison had been glad to have, several, days off. She would be able to spend more time with Lynn.

Allison wanted to take care of, several, errands. She had not wanted to miss a call from Lowell. Allison waited, before she decided to leave home.

Allison got inside her car. The sun had been gleaming.

Within, several, minutes, Allison had begun driving. Allison knew, that there were things that Lynn needed for school. She decided to buy some things for her.

When Allison arrived home, she noticed a car in the drive. As she approached the home, Allison realized that the car belonged to Lowell. He had begun to get out of his car.

Allison approached Lowell.

"I arrived moments ago. I tried to call, but no one answered the phone. I decided to come by, and wait for you to arrive home. I thought we could visit a restaurant for lunch".

Lowell looked at his watch.

Allison agreed to go to lunch with Lowell.

Lowell assisted Allison with her bags. They put away, the items that were bought.

Allison decided to wear a different wardrobe piece. They drove to a restaurant that was minutes away.

Lowell and Allison were soon at the restaurant eating their lunch.

He had not mentioned Daniel or Amy.

Allison had not seen Daniel or Amy, since the wedding, and decided to ask Lowell about them.

Lowell told Allison, that Daniel and Amy were fine. They had been spending their time away.

"They decided to take a week away from home. When I talked to them last, they had been site seeing, and taking photos. Daniel and I enjoy talking with each other, because of our work as photographers. Allison, I' am glad that Daniel and I are able to talk about our knowledge in photography. It gives us new ideas".

Lowell reminded Allison that he had to finish a photo shoot that was scheduled the next morning.

"I made, several, phone calls to let some people know, that I would be returning to work. The agency has, several, projects for me. I have been able to obtain additional work, because of the work I had done in the past".

Allison reminded Lowell, that she felt, he does great with photography.

The restaurant had not been crowded. Allison recognized a woman she worked with in the past. Allison had not expected the woman to recognize her. Lowell and Allison continued their conversation. There were business contracts that had been going well for, several, of his colleagues. Lowell drove Allison and him home.

Things had been quiet, because Lynn had not finished her school day. Allison drove to pick Lynn up from school.

Allison found Lynn waiting for her.

Allison asked Lynn, how long she had been waiting.

Lynn told Allison, that it had been for, several, minutes. She wanted to walk Sammy, when they arrived home.

Allison and Lynn walked along the path. They passed by, several, houses, and decided to walk toward home. They felt the walk had been great.

Lynn thought that Sammy should have a bath.

Allison and Lynn gave Sammy a bath. Lynn was glad.

Allison answered the phone.

It had been Jean wondering how Allison's lunch went with Lowell.

Allison explained the events of their afternoon. Jean knew that Allison was enjoying her time off. They talked for a while.

Jean told Allison, that she had taken Zealand for an appointment that day.

"He is fine. He is older, and I had to be sure that he was eating correctly".

Allison listened to Jean.

That next morning, Allison had been on the phone with Hansen. He was wondering if she would complete a photo shoot that was for a designer named Susan Drumwell. Allison would be part of an event that the designer planned to be part of.

Allison thought that it would be nice opportunity.

Allison called the company to get the details.

When Allison talked with the photographer, he wanted her to meet him that afternoon.

Allison agreed to meet the photographer.

Allison drove over to the photography studio. It was run by, several, employees.

Allison asked for her photographer.

Allison thought that the photo shoot would take, several, hours. It had not ended, until late afternoon.

Allison called Jean halfway through the photo shoot, and asked her to bring Lynn to the building. Allison asked Jean to add food in Sammy's food dish. She explained to Jean, that the photo shoot would last longer than she thought.

Jean had agreed to both.

Lynn was quiet, when she arrived to the building. There were, several, times recently, that Lynn visited a photo shoot Allison was in. She had kept herself busy with her assignment for class.

Allison continued with the photo shoot, and finished a while later. Allison and Lynn enjoyed their time together. Allison and Lynn had made plans afterward, to meet Lowell at his home for dinner. Allison drove them to the home of Lowell.

Allison and Lynn arrived to the home of Lowell.

Lowell was glad to see Allison, and her daughter. Lynn had become more talkative, toward Lowell.

Everything in the home looked, as if it were organized.

Lowell told Allison, that he recently had someone to organize the home.

"That way I would be able to focus on my work".

Lowell asked Lynn about school.

Lynn reminded Lowell, that even without a class pet, things were nice in the new class.

Lowell listened to Lynn.

Lowell enjoyed talking with Lynn. She had a lot to say about her previous class pets, and school.

Lynn paused, as she finished a bowl of butternut squash soup. Squash had been one of her favorite vegetables.

Lynn stopped talking about school. Lowell had not asked Lynn any more questions about school. She remained quiet for a while.

Lowell wanted to discuss the photo shoot that Allison had earlier.

Allison told him, that she thought it had gone well. She worked with a different photographer. The photo shoot had taken longer than Allison thought.

"That is nice Allison".

"Sometimes it takes me a while, to get used to a photo shoot".

Allison told Lowell about the wardrobe pieces that she had worn by the designer. The advertisement would be seen soon.

"When I arrived, the photographer told me that I had the opportunity to be part of the event that was to display his work".

Lowell thought that the event would be a great idea. He poured himself a cup of coffee. Lynn had begun to draw at another table. Time had gone fast to them.

Lowell said that he needed to develop some recent film that he had. He gave Allison a kiss on the cheek, and said goodbye to Lynn, and Sammy.

Lynn enjoyed being around Lowell. She was interested in meeting people. Lynn looked as if she had a long day.

Lynn told Allison, that she had not planned to read that evening. She planned to get some rest.

Allison drove Lynn to school. She had to meet the photographer to complete the photo shoot.

Palmer was waiting, for Allison. He told her, that they managed to accomplish a lot the day before. There were a second series of photos that needed to be completed. By early afternoon, Palmer, and Allison had been ready, for a break.

Palmer left Allison, to make, several, calls. She understood his tight schedule. Work could be hectic for a photographer. Lowell and Allison often talked of this.

Palmer walked toward Allison. He mentioned that another photographer was unable to continue to assist a designer, at an event.

"The designer thought, the photographer was scheduled to assist with the event for, several, days. He is unable to be there the whole time. The photographer was wondering if I would be able to come to the event, and work with the designer. I told the photographer, that I have other work to complete".

Palmer apologized to Allison.

Palmer offered Allison a glass of water.

Palmer handed Allison, a glass of water.

Palmer thanked, Allison for being part, of the advertisement.

It was difficult for Allison to see the roads on her way to pick Lynn up from school. The fall rains left everything obscured. Allison remained cautious. Within an hour, she had become closer to arriving to the school. There were, several, cars in the parking lot.

Lynn noticed Allison, after she blew the car horn.

Allison cautiously drove home. The rain had not let up. Allison and Lynn remained alert. There had been, several, cars, on the road.

Several, moments later, Allison, and Lynn, could see lights gleaming behind their car. Allison could see the lights bouncing behind them, through her mirror. The lights began to flicker, on and off. In case the person in the car had, been trying to get her attention, Allison pulled to the side of the road. Allison and Lynn waited inside, their car.

A woman approached Allison, and Lynn. She looked concerned.

Allison stepped out of the car.

The woman thought, that she heard noise, as if she struck a car.

There had not been any noticeable damage on either car. Allison had reassured the woman, of this.

The woman told Allison, that she had been in a hurry to meet someone.

Allison had a spare flashlight, with her. They continued, to inspect the cars. They were glad, that an accident had not occurred.

Within an hour, Allison, and Lynn, arrived home safely.

Allison called Lowell.

Allison told Lowell, about the encounter Lynn, and she, had with the woman, when coming home.

Before, they ended their conversation, she invited him for dinner. After Allison and Lowell made their plans, she began preparing dinner.

After dinner, everyone was grateful, that the storm had receded.

Lowell stayed, and decided to spend time with Allison, Lynn, and Sammy. He thanked Allison, for inviting him. He visited, for a while.

The phone began to ring.

Allison had not expected a call, from Hansen.

"I wanted to let you know, that the advertisement will be in print, in, several, days. I wanted to congratulate you. Someone from an agency I' am affiliated with, liked your work. The agency wants to use photos that I have of you. They want to use the photo shoot in a newspaper advertisement. I gave them permission, because I was sure, that you would not mind".

Allison told Hansen, that she had not minded the photos being used, in the advertisement. She appreciated, everyone being kind to her. The people around her understood that modeling had been something, that she enjoyed doing.

Allison decided to make a call to Jean, and Sara, and let them know the update.

Jean had been busy working, and told Allison, that she was glad for her. She wanted to say more, but she had to finish sewing material together.

Sara had been working. She was working on a design that was similar, to a gown that she created last year.

"You are working a lot".

Allison had been glad, that she was able to work with Sara for, several, years. She thought Sara, had done a wonderful job, on the many gowns, that she created.

Sara told Allison, that she had been glad, to hear from her.

"We are busy. We are involved, with our careers".

Sara told Allison, that she had been receiving more calls.

"I even have someone answering, my phone. I' am unsure, how much of the work I would be able to complete, on time. There is always, an upcoming deadline".

Allison told Sara, that she knew creating gowns, took time. At this time, she was modeling.

Lowell walked toward Allison, and asked about Jean, and Sara.

Allison told Lowell, that their schedules were busy. At the same time, the designs that Jean and Sara are creating, are progressing.

When Allison awoke the next day, Lynn and she planned to meet the photographer at the photo shoot.

When Allison and Lynn arrived to the photo shoot, Hansen met them there.

Hansen introduced Allison to Sed. She had worked with, several, other models earlier in the day. Sed had been part of another photo shoot.

The first series of photos were completed. More photos needed to be completed. The photo shoot was moving slowly, but Sed and Allison managed to finish, after, several, hours.

Allison had been grateful that everything was present at the location. There was nothing to prolong the photo shoot.

Afterward, Hansen, Allison, and Lynn visited a restaurant. Lynn had been glad for the change of scenery. Hansen had not known what made him decide on the particular restaurant. They continued to enjoy their time.

Hansen, Allison, and Lynn decided it was time to leave the restaurant.

Things went well the next day.

Hansen told Allison, that he had talked with the photographer, and, that she already submitted the photos for the advertisement. He thought the photos had come out well. Allison was welcome to take a look, at them.

Allison told Hansen, that she planned to visit, his office.

The phone rang.

Mark wanted to update Allison on the things going on at the office. Everything had been going well. Mark told Allison, that Darrell decided, to leave the office.

"Darrell decided to go to another firm. He was offered, more compensation".

Allison knew in real estate, it was sometimes difficult, to stay with the same firm.

Mark had been adjusting, to being inside, the office. He told Allison, that he was improving, after his mild stroke.

"Gillian is doing well. I had expected her, to want, to spend more time, at home".

"David has been attempting to show Anne, how to play, board games".

Mark and Allison had a lot to talk about. He told her, that there had not been any other changes in his life. They talked for a while longer, and he decided, that he should finish working.

Allison decided that she would visit Hansen, to see the photos.

Hansen had the photos.

Allison looked through, several, of the photos. She thought that Sed had done a great job, with the photos, she had taken.

"I think that you did a great job, in the photos".

"I' am glad that you had not minded working on this advertisement. I know that you are glad, that you are able to spend more time, with Lynn. I think you are quickly becoming more experienced, at modeling".

Allison visited Lowell, at his studio.

Lowell enjoyed being a photographer. He had been working, as a photographer, since graduating college. He did not mind changes, to his daily schedule.

Allison had been glad, that Lowell had been assisting her. He always gave her good advice.

"Allison, I' am glad, that you are here. I had been thinking about you, moments ago".

Allison thought, that had been kind of Lowell. She watched him, as he continued to finish his work. When Lowell finished developing the last of his film, he came toward Allison.

"I' am done for today. I know that you were, at a photo shoot earlier. I hope that it went well. You are always busy, throughout the day".

Allison enjoyed talking with Lowell. They talked about Lynn. Her daughter had become more self-sufficient, as she became older. Lowell had been glad for Allison.

"Allison, you seem to be used to challenging careers. You do not become overwhelmed with the challenges you have now. There are some things that I could learn from you. My career is hectic and challenging, at times. If you do not capture someone's personality correctly, then it becomes a flawed photo. That is why I have trained for as long as I have, in photography".

"I am glad I decided to continue, in this career. It makes me realize, the opportunities that, comes in life".

Lowell continued to listen to Allison. They spent more time talking, about photography.

Allison noticed the time. She needed to pick Lynn up, from school. Lowell and Allison searched for her car.

A half hour later, Allison picked Lynn up, from school.

Lynn had been glad to see Allison. She knew that they would be going, directly home.

When Allison and Lynn arrived home, Sammy began barking. She wanted to wander around outside.

Lynn had begun ruffling the hair of Sammy.

Lynn wanted to take Sammy for a walk.

Allison agreed that Sammy should go for a walk.

Allison and Lynn gathered everything that was needed, and walked Sammy. She had been home by herself, for most of the day. She had been grateful for the fresh air.

Allison, Lynn, and Sammy arrived home.

Lynn completed her assignment for class.

Lowell called Allison.

It had been a good time for them to talk on the phone.

Lowell told Allison, that he had not known how she kept her life organized.

Allison reminded him, that Jean had not minded assisting her with taking care of Lynn.

"Allison, I' am glad, that we are dating. It is nice that Lynn likes to be around me".

"Lynn understands, that some things in life changes. She does talk with Edgar, often".

"That is a good thing, that Lynn has an opportunity to talk with Edgar. You and I are alike in many ways. I' am glad, that I have an opportunity to be around you. Allison, you are a good listener. I always have a great time talking with you".

Lowell suggested, that Allison, and he make additional plans.

Allison agreed to make plans.

That afternoon, Allison visited with Jean, and Zealand. They were enjoying the warm weather.

Jean had been glad, to see Allison.

"I know that Zealand misses Sammy. They seem, to have a great time together".

Allison and Jean talked about work. Every photo shoot seemed to be different for Allison. Jean spent more time, with her gown designs. She would continue to do that, for a while. Jean liked, that it kept her busy.

"I enjoy, designing gowns".

Allison and Jean continued their conversation. Jean had been glad, that Allison had been doing well, with modeling.

Jean asked, about Lowell.

Allison told Jean, that Lowell had been doing well. He had been making some decisions, on, some upcoming work.

"He is constantly, changing his schedule".

Allison told Jean, about them, visiting a restaurant.

"Lowell wanted to make sure, that we spent time communicating with one another. I' am unsure, if we will become married. That is something that we will talk, about later".

"It is great, that you talk, about, your future together".

Allison noticed, the current design that Jean, was working on. She complemented her. The color of the gown had, been cream.

"I' am glad, that I was able to sell some of my gowns, to some of the boutiques, in the city".

Jean and Allison, walked toward, the inside gate. Dusk was forming.

Jean thought that it would be a good idea, to bring Zealand, inside the home. She may become nervous, outside in the dusk.

Allison wondered if Lowell had decided when, he would begin, several, photo shoots. He had been undecided, when Allison, talked to him, the day before.

Allison drove Lynn to school.

Allison then, attended a photo shoot. It had not lasted long. Allison had no idea, which photos would be used. Each agency had a separate contract.

Allison spoke with the photographer after the photo shoot. She had been glad, that the photographer asked her opinion. Allison decided on the photo, that she thought would be best for the advertisement. She had been wearing her original wardrobe piece that she came to the photo shoot with.

The photographer reminded Allison, that the agency could answer any further questions that she may have.

Hansen called Allison at the studio. He wondered how things had gone.

Allison gave Hansen details of the photo shoot. They ended their conversation. There had been things that Hansen needed to complete, inside his office.

Allison received a call from the agency. They thanked her for wanting to be part, of the advertisement. Allison had been glad that they took the time to call her.

Allison waited for Lynn to arrive home.

Jean told Allison, that she had taken the day off from designing, and did not mind picking Lynn up from school.

When Lynn came through the door, Allison had been on the phone with Mark. He had called her.

"I knew that you would call me soon, Allison. I thought that I would give you a call. I wanted to let you know that everyone is doing well. We are keeping ourselves busy. Gillian stayed home today with Anne. We are preparing David for school in, several, months".

Allison knew that he felt better, after having a mild stroke. Things would improve for him.

Mark asked Allison about Lowell.

Allison told Mark, that Lowell completed a recent photo shoot.

Mark told Allison, that Edgar called the office.

"He plans to come to the office to look at some properties. I do not think that he knew that you worked for Delkes Realty, in the past".

Edgar had not mentioned to Allison, how the search for a house had been going.

Lynn suggested that Allison and she take Sammy for a walk.

Allison put on a sweater.

Allison and Lynn walked along the path. Lynn began a conversation. The class learned some new things. Lynn had been glad of that. Lynn realized that she would see many of her acquaintances, the following year.

Allison was glad, that Lynn was focused at school. Things would be more stable with her activities, once she became older.

Allison reminded Lynn, that they would need to buy, several, things for school, for her.

Lynn began naming school materials, as they arrived back home.

Lynn found her assignment for class, and began working on it. She said that, she understood the work. Lynn talked out loud to Allison, as she figured through it.

Allison had begun to prepare dinner.

Lynn finished her assignment for class.

Allison and Lynn sat on the patio.

Sammy walked outside, toward Allison and Lynn. Sammy sat next to Lynn. She patiently waited for Lynn to go inside, and change her water bowl.

Lynn finished eating, and changed the water bowl, for Sammy. Lynn learned to prepare meals for Sammy.

Sammy remained content.

The evening seemed to go fast.

Lynn drank a cup of warmed tea.

Allison found the building. It was down a narrow road.

Jeremy, a photographer for the photo shoot, asked Hansen if Allison wanted to be part of the photo shoot.

Jeremy introduced Allison, to, several, models. All the models were prepared for the photo shoot. Jeremy gave them pointers. He had shown them, several, facial expressions.

Several, of the models, had their own families. They talked about their families.

Everyone appreciated the photographer being at the photo shoot.

When things became quieter, people began to leave the building. Everyone was happy at the way things turned out with the photo shoot. Their job had been challenging. There were certain techniques that they had to remember.

Before Allison left, she called Lowell.

Lowell had been at his desk, trying to keep up with his work. He told Allison, that he decided to work outside the town for two weeks.

Lowell invited Allison and Lynn to his home for dinner. He would not have to leave for two days.

Allison told Lowell, that she would have to go home, and let Lynn know.

Allison drove toward home. The traffic had been uncongested.

Allison arrived to the home of Jean.

Lynn had been completing an assignment for class.

Allison told Lynn, that Lowell invited them to dinner. It was, at his home.

Lynn was quiet during the ride to visit Lowell.

Allison knew, Lynn most likely, had become nervous. She had not known what to expect.

The dusk was forming, and Allison and Lynn, noticed the lights on the road.

Lowell noticed Allison and Lynn, as they came, into the drive. Lowell opened the front entrance. Lowell had been glad to see Allison, and Lynn. Everything had been prepared for their evening.

They all sat at the table. Lynn decided that she wanted a dessert. She rarely ate sweets.

Lowell asked Allison, about her latest photo shoot.

Allison gave him the details of the day. She hated, that the night was ending.

Lowell enjoyed communicating with Lynn.

Lynn reminded Allison, that Sammy had been alone, for a while.

The next morning, Allison and Lynn ate breakfast together. Lynn drank juice, and Allison drank a cup of coffee. Allison drove Lynn to school.

Allison drove to visit Hansen. They were supposed to have a meeting.

Allison had not noticed Hansen's car outside. She knew that he would arrive soon. Hansen called Allison the night before, to remind her, about their meeting.

Hansen parked next to Allison.

Hansen thanked Allison, for coming to meet with him.

"I wanted us to talk, about your work. We should discuss the direction, you want to continue".

Hansen sometimes held meetings, at his home.

That day, Hansen decided, he would stay inside his office most of the day.

Hansen and Allison talked for a while. He asked her, several, questions. Hansen asked Allison, about being in front of a group of people.

Hansen and Allison drank a cup of coffee.

During the meeting, Hansen talked of, several, business associates. Hansen, and Allison thought, that things, went well.

Jean agreed to pick Lynn up from school. Allison, had not known, how long her day, would be.

When Allison realized, that she would finish her meeting earlier, she called Lowell.

Lowell wanted Allison, and him, to spend time together. He brought the idea up, that they could take a drive.

Allison thought, that taking a drive, would be a great idea.

Lowell met Allison, at her home.

Lowell drove Allison, and him, an hour into the city. It had been before the traffic was congested, from people, leaving work.

Lowell and Allison talked, about things that concerned their relationship. They had not, wanted to change anything. Lowell, and Allison knew, that Lynn would wonder, why they had not become married.

"Allison, I' am unsure of the amount of time, that we will be able to spend, talking while I' am gone. I will be taking, and working, on developing film. I will call you, as often, as I can. I would rather not leave. It would be nice, if you could come, and take photos, with me".

Allison knew that Lowell would have a great time, on the trip. She was glad, that they were close. Allison admired the will Lowell had, to assist others. Lowell enjoyed traveling, with his work.

Allison knew, when she left, that Lynn was with Jean.

Jean knew to expect Allison. She was glad to see her.

"I have been waiting to complete some work. Lynn, and I, decided to give Sammy and Zealand, our attention, for a while. Eventually, Lynn had to complete, an assignment for class. Afterward, she decided, to begin drawing. That is one of her favorite activities".

An hour later, Jean, and Allison continued, to talk. Sammy continued to rest, next to Lynn. Her daughter was drawing, an outdoor beach scene.

Allison drank, from a cup, of coffee.

Jean explained to Allison, her latest design. She was enjoying her dedication, to her designs. Jean added ideas that were similar, to previous designs.

Lynn finished part of her latest drawing. She showed Jean, and Allison.

Allison congratulated Lynn. She had put a lot of work, into the drawing.

Lynn accepted the praise.

Lynn explained that she wanted to add more detail.

"After, I had drawn in the past, now it is easier. I wanted to draw the ocean, because it looks, beautiful in art".

Allison thought that was a wonderful concept.

Lynn continued drawing.

There was more work on the recent design of Jean that needed to be completed.

Sammy had become used to both homes. She had not felt threatened. Sammy may have thought she was related to Zealand. They both enjoyed playing games together.

Jean had nearly, completed her design. The gown had been cream.

Allison knew the familiar work that went, into making the gown. She wanted Jean to be able to work, and decided that it was time, for Lynn, and her, to go home, with Sammy. Lynn managed to complete, her drawing.

Allison and Lynn talked, about their day.

Lynn asked Allison, about Lowell.

Allison told Lynn, that he was doing fine. She reminded her daughter, that he was out of town, taking photos, for two weeks.

Lynn understood why, she had not seen him, in the past two days.

Allison reminded Lynn, that Lowell visits outside the town, every, so often.

Lynn was glad, that everything was going, well for Lowell.

Allison returned, home.

Lynn had gone to school.

Allison expected the phone to ring.

When the phone rang, Lowell had been, on the other line.

Lowell wanted to call Allison, at this time. He told her, that he had been glad, to hear her voice.

Lowell had been, at a photo shoot.

"I thought this, would be one of the best times, to call you. I had not talked with you, since two days ago. I was unsure, of your schedule, today".

Allison told Lowell, that she had not, had any plans.

Lowell told Allison, about some of the work, he was completing. He learned the area. Lowell tried a restaurant, that morning. It was nice.

"I travel verily often, but there are a lot of places, I' am unfamiliar with. I do have people that travel, with me".

As long as Allison had known Lowell, he enjoyed, being able to travel. She knew that, it would have been nice, if she had been able to go on the trip, with him. The conversation ended, when someone wanted the attention, of Lowell.

Lowell told Allison, that someone with the photo shoot, needed to ask him something.

Lowell told Allison, that he would talk, with her soon. There were individuals, with the photo shoot, waiting to ask him questions, about the design, of the photo shoot.

Allison had known, that the photo shoot, was on, a tight schedule. She was glad, that she was able to talk with Lowell. He had been kind to her, and wanted to know the details in her life. At this time, things were busy for Allison and Lowell. They each had their schedule, and it was full.

Allison waited until Lowell hung up, then sat the phone down in the cradle.

After the conversation Allison had with Lowell, she completed, several, recipes for dinner. It had been several, days since she had spent, as much time in the kitchen.

Allison noticed Jean working outside.

Allison assisted Jean with, several, plants that she wanted to add to her garden. Jean had not wanted to add everything, at this time.

Allison updated Jean on the news with Lowell. She told her, that he planned to work for, several, more days. Lowell planned to complete the photos that he needed. He needed certain surroundings for the photo shoot.

Jean and Allison continued their work outside.

Jean talked about her previous marriage with Lenard. They almost decided to have a child. They both realized they had grown apart.

"He wanted to have an answer for everything. I' am able to accept things, the way they are".

Allison could understand the things that changed the marriage of Jean. She remembered the way things were for Edgar and her. Allison remembered the things that they talked about, that brought them to the same conclusion, about their marriage.

When Jean and Allison finished part of their gardening, they could see how things were coming together. She thanked her, for assisting her.

"Every now and again, I decide that I need to change the landscape around".

Jean and Allison worked longer, to finish other parts of the garden.

Sammy was at home.

Zealand remained inside the home.

The skies were darkening.

Jean and Allison managed to finish gardening, before the rain came.

Jean invited Allison inside for a cup of tea.

Zealand had been excited to see Jean and Allison. He became calm, and rested next to them, in the living room. It had been close to the time for Allison to pick Lynn up from school.

Not long after they arrived home, the rain had begun. The rain continued for several hours.

Hansen called Allison to remind her, of the photo shoot, that had been scheduled.

That afternoon, Allison was prepared for work.

Things had been similar as before. Allison met with, several, people, including the photographer. They chose, several, pieces in the wardrobe from the designer. The staff had become demanding on, several, parts of the photo shoot. They managed to get through the difficult parts. The photo shoot continued.

Allison decided to take an hour break.

The photo shoot was completed, after, several, hours.

Things had been similar for Allison the next day.

Allison picked Lynn up from school.

Ms. Bruen told Lynn, that she had done a great job that school year.

Allison had been glad to receive that information.

Lynn told Allison that she would miss her acquaintances.

Allison felt bad for Lynn. She knew that her daughter had enjoyed school. Allison asked her about her plans for the summer.

Lynn mentioned playing Frisbee with Sammy.

Lynn had been glad that she would be able to spend more time with Sammy.

Allison and Lynn arrived home.

Lynn began searching for Sammy. Several, minutes later, she found her napping in the living room.

Sammy awoke.

Lynn ruffled Sammy.

Lynn explained to Sammy, that it had been her last day of school.

Several, moments later, the phone rang.

Edgar had been on the phone.

Edgar planned to take a trip with the peace organization. He wanted to talk with his daughter.

Lynn walked toward the phone, when Allison approached her room. Their daughter had been glad to hear his voice. Lynn explained to Edgar, that it had been the last day of classes.

Edgar congratulated Lynn, on another full year of school.

Allison had been glad, that Lynn had known Edgar, was part, of a peace organization.

Jean was working, in her garden.

Jean allowed Zealand, to wander around outside.

Allison left Lynn, inside the home, as she remained on the phone, with Edgar.

Edgar and Lynn were discussing plans.

Zealand was glad to see Allison, and decided to walk toward her.

Allison continued, walking toward Jean. When Allison approached her, Jean had been, adding a set of seasonal plants, to her garden.

"I feel, as if I have, been outside, too long.

Allison enjoyed the sense of freedom that Jean had. They worked together for a while, before Lynn came toward them, with Sammy behind her. Sammy enjoyed the weather.

Lynn walked toward Allison, and told her, that Mark had been on the phone.

The last Allison talked with him, was when he told her, Edgar had decided, to work with a different office, for the sale, of his home.

Mark talked first. His family and he decided to take a vacation, for, several, days. They were celebrating, that Anne, had begun to walk.

"Anne had begun to walk, last week. We are glad for her. Now I feel, as if I' am able to relax some. Anne is becoming, more self-sufficient".

Allison felt, the same way, as a parent.

"I do think it will be nice, to be able to go, on another vacation. We are going to a beach home that belongs, to Gillian's relatives. They plan to be, at home, this weekend".

"That sounds, nice".

Allison could hear Anne, in the background. Allison told Mark that, several, days ago, had been the last day of school, for Lynn. She had been ready, to begin, the summer.

Mark told Allison, that he had been glad, for Lynn. He had been sure she had learned, some new things, that school year.

Allison agreed with Mark.

Mark realized things, that he had to do, and thought that he should talk with Allison, at a later time.

Allison had not known, the length of time that Edgar, planned to be gone. She assumed, that, Edgar would have, the opportunity, to visit, Lynn, soon. Edgar had known that Allison was dating Lowell.

Lynn was having a great time assisting Jean.

Allison thought that it would be nice, if Lynn and she took Sammy and Zealand, for a walk. They would be able to see, the surrounding area, again.

Sammy and Zealand followed Allison, and Lynn. They walked them, through the, surrounding area. Allison noticed that Sammy, and Zealand, were becoming restless, and, that, was when Lynn, and, she decided, to walk, toward home.

When they arrived home, Jean had been finishing, her gardening.

Jean told Allison, that she had more work that she needed to complete, in her garden. At least, Jean had been able to complete, most of her work, outside. She invited Allison, and Lynn, to join her for dinner. She had been glad, to have them over.

"I have great people, around me".

Jean, Allison, and Lynn, were enjoying themselves.

Allison thought of Lowell. He may have been trying to call her, at home. Allison would call Lowell, later.

Lynn talked about her plans, for the summer.

Jean had been glad, for Lynn.

Lynn told Jean, that, she learned, new things, that school year.

The phone rang. It startled everyone.

Jean answered the phone.

Lowell wanted to talk, with Allison.

"When you had not answered your phone, I knew that you were here".

Lowell explained about, several, meetings, that he had to attend, when he arrived into town. He had been finishing up on some work. There had not been a schedule that he had to remember, as when, he was in town, working.

"I' am simply taking photos, at this time".

Allison reminded Lowell, that she had been having, a busy schedule. She told him, about her meeting, that she had scheduled, the next day.

Lowell asked, about Lynn.

Allison told Lowell, that Lynn had, been fine.

Lowell told Allison, that it had been late, and he was scheduled to awake early. Lowell promised that he would call her, the next day.

Lynn had begun to ruffle Sammy, and Zealand.

Jean was scanning through, several, sketches.

"I plan to go to a gown boutique in the morning. I have to deliver two gowns. This particular boutique has become familiar with my designs".

Allison looked at the sketches, and told Jean, that the gown would look great, when it is completed. She mentioned that in some ways, Jean reminded her of Sara.

Jean understood that as a complement.

Allison told Jean, that she was a great designer.

Allison went, to the photo shoot, alone.

Jean agreed to stay with Lynn, while Allison, was gone.

The photo shoot, had been, a familiar setting. There had been bright lights, in the room.

Allison met, with, the photographer.

A woman remained busy, as she finished setting up, for the photo shoot.

The photo shoot began. Everything was going, as planned.

By the time the photo shoot ended, Allison thought that it, had gone well. She enjoyed herself. Everyone had been kind. Allison had not known when she would, see the photos.

Allison had completed her work, that day.

Jean had been glad, that, Allison returned from the photo shoot. She assumed that it would be, several, hours, before, she was done with work. Jean told Allison, that Lynn had a chance, to talk, with Edgar. He called her, in between, his work.

Lynn had been talking with Edgar more, lately.

Lynn walked toward Allison, with Sammy, walking behind her. She told Allison, that she talked with Edgar. They made plans.

Jean managed to finish gardening, outside.

"I thought that I would have to wait, another day, to finish organizing, my garden".

Allison and Lynn spent more time, outside.

Lowell would not be home, until that next, afternoon. He enjoyed his work as a photographer. Lowell had work to complete, when he returned home. He planned to attend, several, meetings.

Allison was glad that Lowell was to arrive home.

Jean finished cleaning outside. It had taken, several, moments.

Allison fixed dinner for Sammy. She enjoyed the attention.

Lynn had begun to keep herself busy, by drawing.

Sammy remained quiet beside Lynn.

Allison looked through, several, magazines. She enjoyed many of the designs in the clothing.

Allison realized that Sammy had not been walked. She had been patient.

Allison and Lynn finished walking Sammy.

The evening had been cooler, than most recent evenings.

Allison called Sara.

Allison had not talked with Sara in, several, days.

Allison had been glad that she was able to talk with Sara. Similar to Jean, Sara had been working on a gown design. She wanted something completed for a customer. Sara planned to continue working on it for a while.

"I' am glad that I have people contacting me. Another magazine has used one of my gowns for their advertisement. That is something that will be great for me".

Allison had been glad, for the opportunity, to talk with Sara, the evening before. She was prepared to walk Sammy, when the phone rang.

Lowell called, to talk with Allison.

Lowell reminded Allison, that he would be coming home, that next day. There were several, things, left that needed to, be completed. Lowell reminded Allison, that he wished, he was there with her. They talked for, several, moments.

Allison finished her conversation. She realized Lynn, was sleeping.

Allison was looking forward being able to spend time with Lowell.

There was, several, things she needed to complete, for the agency. Allison had been unsure, if they scheduled, a photo shoot for her. She has been having, a busy schedule.

Lowell asked Allison, to meet him at the train station, when he arrived, in town. They were going to go to his home, with his luggage, and equipment.

Lowell told Allison, that he had been glad, that she was able to meet him at the train station. He shared some details with her, of the work he completed.

Lowell told Allison, that he talked, with Daniel, and Amy.

It had been two weeks, since the wedding of Daniel, and Amy.

Daniel and Amy had been, doing well.

Lowell wanted to meet Allison, Jean, and Lynn, for dinner, that evening.

Allison thought that it would, be a great idea.

"I need to make, several, calls, before I leave, to your home".

Allison drove home.

The skies were clear, outside.

Allison returned, home.

Allison decided, on, where to have, dinner.

Allison, Jean, and Lynn, had been waiting for Lowell, when he arrived. He had worn a black, suit jacket.

Allison knew, that Lowell decided to wear the suit, after being away, for, several, days. He wanted to dress, traditional.

When Lowell, Allison, Jean, and Lynn, arrived at the restaurant, they sat at a corner table. Jean had been intrigued, as if she could talk, a while, about, the restaurant. The table had granite, and wooden finishing. Lowell, Allison, Jean, and Lynn had enjoyed the scenery.

Lynn told Jean, that she needed to use the wash room.

They walked to the other side of the restaurant.

Lowell spoke to Allison.

"Will you marry me"?

Allison responded with a yes, to Lowell.

Lowell and Allison waited for Lynn and Jean to return.

Allison told Jean, and Lynn, that Lowell and she would be getting married.

Jean and Lynn congratulated them.

Allison had known that things for the wedding would go great.

Allison knew, that Lynn would continue to remain happy.

Lynn asked her mother to give her details of the wedding.

Allison told Lynn, the details will be planned.

When Allison finished answering Lynn, Lowell put a ring on Allison's left finger.

Lynn had known that Allison would be even happier.

Lowell brought everyone home.

Jean agreed to keep Lynn company, as Lowell and Allison went to a restaurant, for a cup of coffee.

Lowell asked Allison, if she had any ideas on where they should live.

Allison mentioned that they could search for another house together.

Lowell thought buying a different house, would be a great idea.

Lowell and Allison wanted Lynn involved with the details of the wedding. They wanted her to feel, as if the things she had been doing in her life, would not change. Lowell and Allison want the best for Lynn.

Lowell and Allison sat together enjoying their time. They felt as if reality had approached them, and they knew that they had to return home.

Allison had been glad that she met Lowell.

Allison arrived home.

Lynn asked Allison, about the wedding.

Allison told Lynn, that there are details that need to be sorted out with the wedding. She promised her, that she would be able to assist.

Lynn accepted that answer, and congratulated Allison. She had been glad, about the wedding.

Allison assisted, Jean with sewing, a gown. It was part of a bridal collection that she, wanted, to complete.

Jean asked Allison, about her plans, for the wedding.

Allison told Jean, that Lowell, and she, had not completed, the details. She knew they would have an official at the court, marry them. Allison, and Lowell, had not wanted anything elaborate.

Lowell and Allison thought, getting married by the court, will be a good choice, for them.

Jean had not been able to think, of anything, any better for Allison, and Lowell.

Jean planned to assist, with the details.

"I know that everything, will work out for the best. The both of you will, be happy".

Jean and Allison talked longer.

Allison thought that she should go home, and prepare dinner. Allison, and Lynn, was expecting Lowell, over, for dinner.

The dinner had been, completed.

Lowell arrived, with a bottle, of wine. Allison, Lowell, and Lynn kept themselves entertained. Their evening had been, going well.

Lowell asked Allison, about the meeting she had earlier, with Hansen.

Allison told Lowell, that her meeting had, gone well. She would not have any photo shoots, scheduled, for the next, several, weeks. Allison thought that, it was a nice change.

Lowell stayed as long as he could. He mentioned that he contacted a realtor. He would begin to see what houses are available.

Allison knew that the marriage would be a change for Lynn.

The dinner had been cleared, since the past hour.

Allison observed, as Lynn began to keep Sammy entertained. They had a great time together. Lynn had the summer off from school.

Allison was glad that Jean agreed to keep Lynn company.

Allison hoped that the photo shoot would be completed that day. She was wearing a suit by a designer she was unfamiliar with. Allison followed the instructions of the photographer. The camera was flashing, and the photographer took over a dozen photos. He had been content with the photos.

The photographer had gone over some details with Allison.

The photo shoot had been completed.

Allison thanked the photographer.

Allison arrived home.

Lynn was drawing.

Allison called Lowell at his office.

Lowell was glad to hear the voice of Allison.

Lowell told Allison about his day. It had been long. Lowell had two meetings. The individuals involved with the advertisement, wanted to give him the details of the photo shoot. They wanted things a certain way.

Allison assumed that Lowell was concerned. She told him, that the advertisement will go well.

Allison and Lowell talked about the house.

Lowell found a house that they will like.

Allison listened. She thought that it was a good choice.

Allison and Lowell talked about the house in detail.

The realtor had been familiar with the property.

Lowell reminded Allison, where the office, was located.

Lowell and Allison discussed plans, to talk with the realtor, midweek.

By this time, Allison wanted to let Lowell finish his work, for the day. He planned to meet her, at her home, for dinner.

Allison went to look for Lynn, to see if she wanted to assist her in preparing the dinner.

Lynn told Allison, that she had not minded, assisting her, with dinner.

Within a short time, the dinner had been, prepared.

Lynn had not, asked Allison, about the, wedding plans. She realized, that she would, know, soon enough.

Allison waited during dinner, before she told Lynn, that, Lowell, and she, planned to buy a house. Once they buy the house, then, they would have the wedding dinner, there.

Lynn was glad, about, the news. She said that, she wanted everyone, to be happy.

"We have been waiting, a while, to settle, these plans. We will all continue, to discuss things, together".

Allison told Lynn, that Lowell, and she, planned, to buy the house, before school began.

"We have plenty of time, to move".

Lynn understood the, moving plans.

Lynn mentioned that, it was nice to do something, different, that summer.

Within an hour, they all assisted, in cleaning up. The cleaning, had not taken, them long.

Afterward, Lynn joined Lowell, and Allison, as they thought, out ideas, for the wedding. She knew that, they planned to get married, at the courthouse. Allison would wear a gown that Sara, created. By the time they, finished discussing their ideas, Lynn, had been glad. Lowell had, an appointment, that next afternoon, and thought, that he, should go.

"My work, always, keeps me busy".

Lowell apologized, for having, to leave.

Lynn told Allison, how happy, she had been. She wondered, what her new bedroom, would look like.

Allison told Lynn, that she had been unsure, what her bedroom, would look like. They would, visit the house, soon.

Allison and Lynn decided to take care of some errands, and buy items at a local store.

Allison and Lynn arrived home.

Allison and Lynn decided to bring Sammy into the city to visit the dog groomer.

Sammy was calm. She, must have become used to the visits with the groomer.

"I' am glad that Sammy is being patient. It has been a while, since she has been in the city".

Sammy was grateful for the visit.

Allison was driving Lynn, Sammy, and she home. It would take them a while. Lynn ruffled Sammy. They had been having a great time.

Allison looked through some photos Lowell had previously taken.

Allison and Lynn waited on Lowell to arrive. He planned to drive Allison and Lynn to meet with the realtor. He had available time, in the midafternoon.

The woman was knowledgeable.

The house was, as Lowell described it. They had plenty of space. Lynn had been anxious to see her new bedroom. The realtor explained the main details of the house. The realtor had given the information, on what it would take to keep Lynn enrolled at her same school. The realtor knew that Lowell and Allison planned to sell their current homes.

The realtor agreed to meet Lowell, and Allison, whenever, they, were ready. She would, make her schedule, available, for them. She had not, thought, they would have, too many details, to worry about, in purchasing, the house. The realtor had, recently been showing, several, properties. No other family had, been interested, in the house, at, this time.

Lowell, thought that Allison, and he should, go ahead, with, the purchase. Lowell, Allison, and Lynn, left the house. Lowell began to drive, them home.

Allison updated Jean, on the news, with the house. She told her, that, they agreed to go forward, with, the purchase. Jean had been, glad, for, the family.

The wedding ceremony had, already, been planned.

"It is, in, several, weeks".

Allison agreed, with Jean. The wedding ceremony, would, be soon.

Lowell called Allison.

He said that he had already taken care of the details, with the realtor. She told him, that the, house, would be ready, within, the coming weeks.

Allison thought that was good news. The house would be available in, several, weeks.

Within, several, weeks, their move was, nearly finished.

Lynn had worn a white dress, that, Jean made for her. Allison had worn a cream dress that Sara made.

A driver had come, to pick up, Allison, and Lynn.

Lowell met them, at, the courthouse.

There had been Mark, and, his family, also, at, the courthouse. Sara and Jean joined.

The ceremony had, been short. Everyone waited outside, and congratulated Lowell and Allison, as they, left the building. The driver drove, Allison, Lowell, and Lynn home. The, several, people that they invited would meet them, at their home, for dinner.

Lowell talked.

"I' am glad, that the people that are close to us will be, at the dinner".

Allison agreed.

When Lowell, Allison, and Lynn arrived home, the dinner table had already, been set. The home had, been decorated. There had been centerpieces in the dining room, where the guest, would be.

Daniel and Amy had brought, Andrew, with them. Amy had become pregnant, since Daniel, and Amy were married.

The dinner was going well.

Lowell and Allison would not have, wanted, anything different.

Lowell had planned to take, several, days off, from his schedule. He had not planned to take any work related phone calls.

The evening had gone fast. Everyone there wished them well.

Sara and Daniel said something in regards, to the bride and groom. The guests waited, as long as they could. The evening had, become late. Sara and her family had been some of the last people to leave.

The guests enjoyed themselves.

The next morning Allison, Lowell, and Lynn had taken a walk together near their home. They had not seen anyone outside. After an hour, they walked toward the home. There had been cleaning that needed to be done, from the night before. The guests were glad to be able to see the home for the first time.

Allison received a call from Sara.

Sara told Allison, that it had not taken her as long as she thought to reach the city. She wanted to let Allison know, that she had a great time at the wedding. Sara had more work that needed to be completed with her designs.

Later that afternoon, Allison and Lynn took Sammy for a walk.

Lynn mentioned that she felt that Sammy was adjusting to her new home.

Allison told Lynn, that they would take Sammy to visit Zealand. She thought that they would miss each other. The family was no longer in as close proximity to Jean and Zealand.

When Allison, Lynn, and Sammy, arrived home, Lowell had been on a phone call with someone familiar to them. Allison had known that Lowell planned to take, several, days off from work. He held his hand over the mouth piece.

"Amy has gone into labor. Daniel is calling from the hospital. Everything is going fine".

Lynn ruffled Sammy. She had become even older.

Lowell ended his phone conversation. He asked Allison, when they should visit Daniel and Amy.

Lowell, Allison, and Lynn decided to go to the hospital. They drove toward the city. Lowell, Allison, and Lynn had a late lunch at a restaurant.

Lowell, Allison, and Lynn arrived to the hospital.

Daniel met them at the main entrance. They walked, toward, a wind in the hospital.

"I' am glad, things are going well. I know that it is the first labor, for us. The doctor said that she was glad, that the delivery is moving smoothly".

Lowell, Allison, and Lynn waited in the lobby at the hospital.

Periodically Daniel, had come out to the lobby, and let them know, how Amy had been doing.

Daniel came into the lobby, after, several, hours, and told Lowell, Allison, and Lynn, that the baby had been born. They would name her, Josephine.

Daniel brought the baby inside the lobby, so that Lowell, Allison, and Lynn could see her. He held her, and then brought her to Amy.

Daniel returned later, and talked, with everyone.

Before Lowell, Allison, and Lynn left the hospital, Daniel told them Amy, and he would talk with them soon. Lynn had begun to feel, as if, she had a long day.

Lynn drifted to sleep, through the ride home. She had a busy day.

Lowell had been glad, that everything had been going well for Daniel, Amy, and their family.

Allison and Lowell talked, about, their own lives. They made a decision, that they would accept the idea of a child, if Allison, had become pregnant.

Hansen had been patient as he waited for Allison. He told her, that he had been waiting for, several, moments. They were supposed to have a meeting over lunch about her next project. Hansen and Allison had not talked since the wedding. He congratulated her on her marriage.

Hansen told Allison that he had a great time at the wedding.

Hansen handed Allison a wrapped box. It was a picture frame.

"I thought that maybe you could use it for your wedding photos".

Allison thanked Hansen.

Hansen immediately, had been prepared to go through the meeting. He explained to Allison, that there had been, several, advertisements that would be great for her. Hansen told Allison, that lately, he had been busy. He had more work than usual.

Allison was glad, that Hansen and she were able to meet. They felt, as if they had known each other for a long time. Hansen and Allison continued to drink coffee. They noticed the people walking by.

Hansen continued where he left off. He told Allison, that he would make some calls. He would keep her updated on modeling opportunities.

"I always want to make sure I do my job".

Hansen told Allison, that he had some photos that he needed to take. He had planned to go into the city for, several, hours, but hopefully he would have his work completed.

"Things usually do go fast. I have, several, people that will meet me, to assist me through an upcoming project".

Hansen was glad, he had assistance.

Within an hour, Hansen and Allison had their plans completed.

They ended their meeting. Allison had begun to drive toward the city. Allison met the photographer at a previous photo shoot. He worked as a photographer, for many years. The photographer had been setting up his equipment.

Allison walked around for a while. It was time for her to begin work. Allison had become used to the familiarity with photo shoots. The photographer was able to complete, several, scenes, before they took a break.

The photo shoot continued.

On this particular photo shoot, Allison had worn, several, different designs of clothing.

The photo shoot slowed down, after the scenes that would be used, were decided on.

On one set of photos, Allison looked, as if she were taking photos with her family. She visualized the times she spent with her daughter.

The set designers were content with their work. Allison was able to end her day at the photo shoot.

Allison thought about Lynn, as she drove home. She passed an art gallery. Allison thought that Lynn would enjoy visiting the gallery one day. She enjoyed art.

Allison decided to bring Lynn and Sammy with her to visit Jean and Zealand. It had been, several, days since Jean saw them. Lowell had been at work.

Zealand had been happy to see Allison, Lynn, and Sammy. His facial expression looked, as if, he wondered, where, they had gone.

Zealand walked toward Lynn, to be ruffled.

Jean had been able to catch up with Sammy, as he walked toward Allison and Lynn.

Allison told Jean, that she decided to bring Lynn and Sammy with her.

Jean had been glad for Allison, that she was married.

"I almost feel as if I' am here to pick up Lynn. I guess that is not the case".

Allison and Lynn walked inside the familiar home with Jean. They drank a cup of tea with her.

Allison told Jean about her latest photo shoot.

Jean asked Allison, if Lowell, Lynn, and she, planned to take a vacation as a family.

Allison told Jean, they had not, for their wedding. She told her, that eventually, they would.

The time went fast. The time everyone was spending together, was great.

Jean had some ideas for some designs. She asked Allison, for her opinion.

Jean and Allison talked more about one particular design.

Jean told Allison, that it was similar to a dress that she had worn, several, years ago. The gown had a sheer back. The dress had been in her closet.

"I did enjoy making the gown".

Jean and Allison talked more about the design, before Allison noticed the time. She knew that Lynn, and she, needed to go home.

"I would not want Lowell to wonder where we are. He is waiting for us".

Lowell, Allison, and Lynn spent time together.

Sammy had been watching Allison, and Lynn paint. Lynn walked towards Allison, to show her the work that she had completed. She paused, and began to think a moment, before she talked.

"I was wondering, since Sammy is further away from Zealand, if we could get another dog? That way she could have someone to play with at home".

Lowell looked at Allison, before she talked.

Allison told her daughter, that Lowell, and she, needed to think about the idea.

"We would enjoy the idea, but it is not that simple".

Lynn understood the answer. She agreed that she would wait for them to let her know. Lynn wanted to continue with her art. She had wanted to spend more time painting. Lynn kept herself preoccupied.

While Lynn worked, Lowell, and Allison, looked through some photos he had recently taken. He wanted the whole photo shoot, to be outdoors. Lowell wanted to utilize a beach in the scene. The client had not wanted the whole photo shoot outdoors. A small part, of the photo shoot would be outdoors.

Allison admired the work of Lowell. She enjoyed the times that she had sat down, and looked through his portfolio of photos.

Lowell and Allison were preoccupied, and had not noticed Sammy taking a nap in the kitchen. She had done that, when she wanted some food, or water, added to her bowls, and everyone one around her had been busy.

When Allison added water to Sammy's bowl, she awoke, and walked toward it.

Lynn finished painting, and had begun looking through an assignment, that she had completed in class.

Allison told Lynn, that they could visit the animal shelter in the city, and she could look for another dog.

Lynn was glad, that Sammy would be around anther dog.

As promised, the next morning, Allison drove Lynn and her into the city.

The animal shelter personnel had been waiting for someone to visit.

Lynn explained, that Allison and her, wanted to buy another dog.

The woman told Lynn, that it was a great idea.

The woman, Allison, and Lynn found a Cavalier King Charles Spaniel. He was a boy. Allison and Lynn agreed they both liked him.

The woman asked Lynn the name that she wanted to give him.

Lynn told the woman, Wilson.

Allison and Lynn visited Joyce Eagleston, with Wilson. She had been able to groom Wilson, because she had availability.

Allison and Lynn talked on the way home.

When Allison and Lynn arrived home, Lowell had been waiting for them.

Wilson enjoyed being around Sammy.

Lowell congratulated Lynn on the new family dog.

Lynn told Lowell the name of the dog.

Lowell, Allison, and Lynn spent time playing games with Sammy and Wilson. Lowell suggested that they be able to wander around outside before dinner.

Lowell, Allison, and Lynn went outside with Sammy and Wilson. Lowell threw a ball around, and Wilson began chasing it. He had been adjusting to his new home.

Lowell assisted Allison with preparing dinner.

The family had almost finished with their dinner, when the phone rang.

Sara had been on the other end.

Sara wanted Allison to know, that she had decided to sell her boutique. She sold the remaining gowns that she had. Sara decided she would work from home.

"I rather focus more on designing. Lately, I have been having a difficult time with my boutique".

Sara reminded Allison, that she had enjoyed having the boutique.

Allison told Sara, that maybe it had been the correct decision for her. She asked her, to keep her updated.

Sara reminded Allison, that she had to complete some details. She had expected that the process of leaving the boutique would not be too complicated.

Allison had not learned what made Sara decide to sell her boutique.

Allison ended the conversation with Sara.

Lowell and Lynn had been ruffling Sammy and Wilson.

Allison mentioned to Lowell, Sara's plans with her boutique. She had given him, the details, that she had given her. Sara planned to continue working on her designs. She continued, to spend time with her family, while she owned her boutique.

Sara had been older than Allison, by, several, years.

Lowell enjoyed the time, his family, and he was spending together.

"Lynn has adjusted to being around me. The difference now is that I' am around Lynn and you, longer than a family dinner".

Lowell mentioned, that he thought they should wait a while, before doing any family travels. He had to meet a prospective client soon.

An agency asked him to complete a photo shoot. He knew that working with the agency would go well. He worked with the gentleman in the past. Lowell had created a series of photo shoots for the gentleman. They would meet with, several, other people.

Lowell had called over to the agency to confirm the details of the photo shoot. He was glad that he had been able to assist the agency.

When Lowell arrived home, Allison had moments before, finished a conversation with Sara. They talked, again that day. Allison told Lowell, that this time they had more time to talk. She even updated her on her family. Sara was glad, that Lynn was able to get another dog.

That morning, Allison had also been able to talk with Mark. He had been working and spending time with his family. Since the scare with his mild stroke, he managed to work less hours.

"Some of the prospective clients keep me busy".

Allison told Mark, that she had been glad for him, for not allowing himself to work longer hours. He had been grateful that he had wonderful people around him.

Lowell finished his work early.

Allison suggested that Lowell, Lynn, and she could walk Sammy and Wilson. They had not been able to see much of the surroundings, since moving in their home.

Sammy and Wilson were glad to be back outside.

Within a short time, Lowell, Allison, Lynn, Sammy, and Wilson passed several houses. The houses were similar to their home. Sammy and Wilson wandered around in an open area. When Sammy and Wilson became restless, the family walked toward their home. They finished their walk.

Sammy and Wilson were calm, when they arrived home.

Sammy and Wilson sat next to Lynn as she painted.

Lowell decided to make, several, calls.

Allison was expecting to talk with Hansen. They were going to talk about upcoming modeling work that she wanted to be part of. Allison had not worked for, several, weeks.

Lowell continued to talk on the phone. He ended his last conversation. Lowell realized, that he would be working, that next day.

The family ate dinner.

Allison decided to call Sara. She wondered the plans she had, to relocate her things home.

Sara told Allison, that she had been able to complete more designs at home. She hired, several, people to assist her with the move. She asked them to bring some items to her home, while she donated others. Sara planned to convert another room into a studio.

Sara reminded Allison, that she had not come to visit her in a while in the city.

Allison knew that Sara had not been able to formerly spend time with Lowell.

Sara mentioned that her family had not taken a vacation together in a while. Everyone had been busy doing their own activities. They ended their conversation, and Allison had a much clearer idea of the plans Sara had with her designing business.

Lowell had been working at home most of the afternoon. Allison decided that Lynn and she would drive into the city to take Lynn shopping for school. It was close to the time the school year would begin.

Lynn found wardrobe pieces that she liked.

Allison and Lynn were gone for, several, hours in the city. Allison and Lynn had gotten the things that they needed. They even managed to buy something for Sammy and Wilson.

Lynn mentioned to Allison that she had not minded shopping for the upcoming school year. The upcoming school year she would enjoy wearing her new clothes.

Allison and Lynn decided to have tea, before they returned home.

The drive away from the city went fast. Lynn had not said as much during this particular drive home. Allison came into the drive. Allison had known that Lowell had been home. Allison and Lynn were ready to be inside.

The family began eating dinner. Lowell told Allison and Lynn about his day. He had been on the phone again for part of the afternoon. Lowell had not known where he would be working. There had been, several, people that he might be working with. Lowell knew, several, dates that he would be working. He had planned that next day to take several photos. There was a photo shoot Lowell had to take for a designer. He had been glad that he was able to work with the designer.

"I know things will go smoothly. I will be working for most of the day".

Lynn had a long day.

Allison was glad that Lynn was looking forward to her upcoming school year. Allison had not known what work she would complete with modeling.

Allison had a meeting with Hansen. Lynn agreed to come, with her.

Lowell had gone, to complete, another photo shoot.

Hansen had been at his office. He had some other things, to do, that day. Hansen asked Allison, what type of work, she had been interested completing? He reminded her, that there were some designers that would be completing, current advertising.

After, Allison gave Hansen her ideas he told her they were great.

Before Allison left, Hansen asked her, how she had been doing? He was not around Allison as often, once, she had, become remarried.

An hour later, Allison, and Lynn, left the meeting.

Allison drove them home.

Lynn asked Allison, several, questions about her schedule, and career.

Allison answered, as best, she could.

Allison and Lynn arrived home.

Sammy and Wilson began walking, toward Allison, and Lynn.

Allison realized that Lowell had, not been home. She knew that he was working. Allison reminded herself, about the photos that he, had to take. She asked Lynn, if she wanted to assist her, in preparing dinner.

Lynn wanted to assist Allison with dinner.

For the next hour, Lynn followed instructions, as Allison, and she, prepared dinner.

Lowell, Allison, and Lynn sat, and ate dinner.

Lowell put things away, as Allison, and Lynn spent time, with Sammy, and Wilson.

Lynn continued to keep herself entertained, while Lowell and Allison looked at photos he had taken. They talked for a while. Lowell usually gave the photos back to the agency, after he finished looking through them.

Lowell and Allison knew that their career choice had not been typical. Not many people would understand their knowledge of modeling and photography. Lowell and Allison drank, a cup of coffee, before putting away the photos.

Lowell kept a similar routine, as he had, for, the past week.

Allison and Lynn waited for Jean. She planned to visit them, with Zealand.

When Jean and Zealand arrived, Lynn had been, in the middle, of painting. Jean had been glad to see them. She had not seen, Allison, Lynn, and Sammy, in, several, weeks. Zealand recognized the familiar surroundings.

Sammy, Wilson, and Zealand began to wander around outside. They continued to keep themselves, preoccupied.

Jean had a lot to talk about, as she talked of her newest, gown design. She continued to have a great time designing. It had become easier for Jean. She wanted something that had been original, with her latest design. Thus far, Jean managed to do that. She enjoyed, taking part, in fashion events. Jean spent a while, at the home.

Jean thought that Zealand and she should, go home. She had a great time visiting them. Jean had, several, things that she, needed to complete, that day. She told Allison, that she would visit again, soon.

Jean and Zealand left, the home.

Allison began to clean.

Allison completed, the work that she, wanted.

Allison thought that it was nice of Jean, to visit. There had been, several, things that Jean, needed to get done, that she had planned to complete.

Lowell, Allison, and Lynn ate dinner. Allison told Lowell, about the visit, from Jean, and Sammy. She told him, that Jean asked, about him.

After the dinner, Lynn, had gone to, her room.

Lowell asked Allison, if he should take the opportunity to take photos outside the town.

"It would be for a week".

Allison reminded him, that it was his decision. Everyone would support him, if chose to go.

Lowell planned to think about it for a while.

The next day, Allison, and Lynn went to a meeting with Hansen. They met him at a restaurant. He had decided on it, because he would be meeting someone else later that afternoon, near the restaurant.

Hansen arrived with a portfolio. There had been models advertising for designers. Hansen had not had a lot to say. He wanted to show Allison some of the work in the portfolio.

Lynn attempted to keep herself preoccupied. She finished eating. Lynn was intrigued by the meeting. She enjoyed being at the restaurant.

Hansen had a lot of good ideas, when he was working.

"It is nice, that with photography, there are always opportunities to display your talent. It is nice to be able to see the finished project".

It had been something, that Lowell, and Allison talked about often.

When Hansen, and Allison, finished their meeting, Lynn was restless. She became alert, by the time they arrived to the car.

Lowell had already been home, and was glad that his photo shoot had gone well. He was able to get the photos that were needed. Lowell felt everyone worked hard. He had worked with some new people that he had not in the past worked with. Lowell told Allison, that he had not talked with Daniel and Amy in, several, days. The family was probably getting used to the new baby.

Everyone was glad to be home. Lowell decided that he would take some photos outside of town. He would contact, several, people, and planned to leave in, several, days. The trip would last a week.

Allison and Lynn had been glad for him. He had not wanted to travel as often.

Lowell, Allison, and Lynn decided to take a walk with Sammy and Wilson.

There was a short time left, to the summer vacation that Lynn had.

About the Author

Valerie Lee J enjoys writing about families and romance. She has written other books titled *The Changing Room*, *Fallen Artist*, and *Rider*.